It Should Have Been Gold

The Silent Runner Speaks

by Calvin Smith
and Kerry Kendall

Editor: Marilyn Briant

Library of Congress Number: 2015960994

NDYG Publishing
Poinciana, FL

ISBN-13: 978-0-9970888-0-9

Printed in the United States.

We regret we have been unable to find the source of the trophy picture at the end of chapter 4. All other pictures, unless already credited, are courtesy of Calvin Smith and the Smith family.

Dedication

I'd like to dedicate this book, and my story of clean running, to my dear mother, who worked so hard to raise me to be the man I am. And to the wonderful young athletes I coach, as well as all the athletes that are out there working hard and running drug-free, regardless of the pressure to use drugs. They choose not to, despite all the fame that winning would bring.

Contents

It Should Have Been Been Gold

The Silent Runner Speaks

Acknowledgements

We were lucky enough to have the keen eye of editor Marilyn Briant to tidy up our words. She is the author of *Arms Out* and *The Leopard and the Mouse*.

The U.S. Olympic Archive presented by Gordon Crawford, at the Paley Center for Media in New York City, was our source for the Olympic telecast information. Mark Ekman and his staff set us up to watch it again, over 30 years later. For television history and current events, the Paley Center is worth a trip.

The hospitality of General Manager Gene Nicotra Jr. at the Hotel Pennsylvania was very much appreciated during a snowy weekend of research. It's right across the street from Madison Square Garden! And a big thanks to Gene's mother, Lynn Nicotra, for connecting us.

The Hetrick family (Bill, Marilyn, Jitney and Ed) of RE/MAX Alliance in Clinton, Mississippi, graciously provided accommodations for all work done in the Magnolia State.

The Mississippi Sports Hall of Fame was instrumental in getting the authors together before this book was even an idea. Bill Blackwell, Rick Cleveland and staff have a classy operation at the HOF in Jackson. Calvin Smith was inducted in 2014.

We appreciate the input and fine memories of track coaches Russ Rogers and Wayne Williams.

And of course, thanks to the Smith families of both Mississippi and Florida for providing the history. Angie, Candy and Mrs. Smith had the stories that made Calvin remember.

Forward by Harvey Glance

3-time Olympian and Olympic Gold Medalist

Calvin Smith is no doubt one of the greatest sprinters to lace up spikes. We trained together and competed for a decade. He was a natural athlete who opposed drug use as well as myself. He was much accomplished without the use. He will do go down in my opinion as one of the top 5 greatest sprinters of all time.

Harvey Glance currently coaches Olympic sprint champion, Kirani James.

Preface by Calvin Smith

During my entire running career, as I represented the United States in some of the biggest track and field contests in the world, I never took drugs. Not to get stronger. Not to run faster. Not to recover from an injury. Never.

I loved running, but retiring was easy. I had enough of the dirty business of track and field under the International Amateur Athletic Federation (IAAF). I went on with my life and almost forgot about all the hypocrisy and deceit in that world. What I really mean is cheating. (Yes, doping is cheating and I know athletes were doping.) Then in 2012, I was asked to take part in the 30/30 project, 9.79, a documentary for ESPN and it brought up all the old memories and all the old frustrations. It made me think that it's time to tell the real story.

I believe that most of the athletes who beat me on the track were on drugs. I want that to be written down before I pass on because I have children, and someday, I hope to have grandchildren. Everyone has a legacy. When my medals get handed down, the story behind them should too.

I don't understand how so many others held their heads up high, and stood on those Olympic podiums, when they won by cheating. Sadly, I've watched this sham for over thirty years and I don't see an end in sight.

I'm about to ruin my reputation of being the nice, quiet guy on the team. Truthfully, I didn't talk about doping during my running career for fear of being blacklisted. I saw it happen to others. But I'm off the track now and I run on my own terms.

I'm speaking out because the next generation of Olympians deserves better. Not only is my son, Calvin II (Calvin Two), a clean runner on our national team, but there are others competing the right way also. These young athletes need our support. I've never seen any evidence of the IAAF applauding the clean runners for their choices, so I will, by telling what I know. Maybe it will help.

This is my story from inside the world of track and field. It's both factual and opinionated.

The infamous bronze is currently on display at the Alabama Sports Hall of Fame where I was inducted in May of 2016.

1

Shut Up and Take the Bronze

It was Monday, Sept. 26, 1988. Another warm, clear, summer day in Seoul, South Korea. It was much like it was on the day of the race, just seventy-two hours ago. I was summoned to the scene of the crime, Olympic Stadium, to get a medal for coming in third in the 100 meters. The U.S. sprint coach, Russ Rogers, came with me. I was so hurt and angry that I don't actually remember who else took part in this so-called ceremony.

Six athletes had already been disqualified from these Games because of positive drug tests. Canadian Ben Johnson was the seventh, and most notorious, because his disqualification came after he had won the gold medal in my event with a new world record time of 9.79 seconds. When the urine sample he produced three hours later tested positive for the steroid stanozolol, he was stripped of that gold medal and the new world record was erased from the books before the ink was dry.

I had actually crossed the finish line in fourth place behind Ben Johnson, Carl Lewis (USA) and Linford Christie (Great Britain). With Ben out, the rest of us moved up. I, however, was the only clean runner among the medalists.

I was going to get a bronze medal at the XXIV Summer Olympics. It would have been an honor, if I didn't already know the secrets hiding behind the grand Olympic curtain. I deserved the gold and they knew it. They also knew that I knew it. Yet nobody said anything. The cost would have been too great for all of us. If they talked, a worldwide audience would have known how drugs had fueled so many of the athletes at these games. The Olympics would have become a joke.

NBC had a lot at stake. They bid some outrageous amount, like $300 million dollars for the broadcast rights. The network, its sponsors and the sponsors of individual teams and athletes could have pulled millions of dollars of support.

If I talked, it would have cost me everything. Running was how I made a very good living. I had a career that I loved and a wife and two kids to support. I kept quiet too.

Long after that race in Seoul, Carl Lewis admitted he failed three drug tests during the U.S. trials for the 1988 Games. Those tests were not made public at the time. He said he didn't know a stimulant was in the herbal supplement he was taking.

Now, I wasn't in the room, so I don't know what the U.S. Olympic Committee (USOC) actually said to Carl, but I imagine it went something like this, "That's okay, Carl. We know you didn't mean to get caught taking performance-enhancing drugs. And since you're our national poster boy for track and field, we'll let it slide. But don't do it again. Good luck in Seoul." They probably finished with a slap on the wrist and sent Carl out to run again, cautioning him to watch his herbal intake so close to race day. That's what I imagine happened.

The International Olympic Committee (IOC) let Linford Christie of Great Britain off the hook for testing positive for the stimulant pseudoephedrine right after the race. He told them he didn't know that it was in his ginseng tea. The IOC decided to forgive him for that lack of knowledge. But it was a split decision. It was getting harder to cheat, but not impossible.

Carl Lewis's time in this race in Seoul, was 9.92. Linford Christie came in at a chemically-enhanced 9.97.

Due to Ben Johnson's drug test at this Olympics, his world record of 9.83 in the 100 meters at the 1987 World Championships in Rome would also be scrapped.

The previous world record was mine at 9.93, unaided by chemicals. And it still should have been the world record after the Games in Seoul, if life were fair. But in track and field, it isn't, it's doped-up, or rather, performance-enhanced.

There's currently a three-year statute of limitations on changes to the Olympic record. After that, they're set in stone, for now anyway.

The official Olympic record shows me in third place but I was the moral victor. I was the fastest runner in the world who did not damage his body or cheapen the sport with human growth hormone or steroids or blood doping or even a pre-race jolt of caffeine. If I had dropped dead on the track after I crossed the finish line, my autopsy would show no trace of drugs. I didn't want to have to go that far to prove it, but take it from me, I'm one of the few Olympic athletes who could.

Ben Johnson's positive drug test at the Games was no surprise to me. The only surprise was that the

IOC decided to punish him and make it public. I knew other athletes had tested positive in the past and nothing was done about it. I wondered why now, and why on the biggest international stage? Was the IOC trying to make a point? Why choose Ben Johnson to take the hit? Why not choose a weightlifter or a swimmer? Ben had recently had a hamstring injury. Did he load up to compensate? Was Ben's test somehow too positive to hide?

From his three positive tests at the U.S. trials, we knew that Carl Lewis was doping too. That was also no surprise. I don't think the gold medalist had run on pure athletic ability for many years. (It wasn't a secret inside the world of track and field.) He should have gotten a three-month ban that would have made him ineligible for these games.

Linford Christie hung on to his silver medal despite his ginseng tea mistake. I imagine the discussion by the IOC members, before the split decision came down on that excuse, centered more around Ben Johnson than ginseng tea.

The IOC couldn't afford to lose two of the top three finishers in the headline race of the games. If they did, someone probably would have spilled the beans on Lewis too. And, oh no, how could Calvin Smith walk away with the gold when the international audience saw him finish fourth behind the drug runners? We couldn't have that now, could we? There's your split decision maker on Linford's tea. That's how I imagine he got away with it.

As for me, no one actually said it, but it was clear, "Shut up and take the bronze." It was going to be hard to do that, knowing it should have been gold.

When Coach Rogers and I arrived at the stadium, an official from the IOC was waiting for us, just past the spectator entrance and ironically far away from the finish line of my race. I couldn't even see the track from here. We were under the bleachers. No podium. No flags. No media. Even the stadium janitors seemed to be on their lunch break.

I guess putting the bronze medal around my neck in front of too many witnesses would only serve to highlight how the IOC finally hung an athlete out to dry for cheating. Yep, too much ceremony. The official simply handed it to me in its box, as if he were returning something I had dropped. I resisted the impulse to drop it again, or to even open it, or to tell him where to shove it. I had been playing this game for so long that this was just another day at the office.

I'm glad Coach Rogers was there. He knew I was the fastest runner in the world who did not cheat. He saw the injustice and let me know he felt sorry for me, missing out on a real ceremony. It helped, a little.

Since I was now an Olympic medalist from the U.S., in the middle of the story of the day, NBC wanted me for an interview during their prime-time coverage. This was sports entertainment and even though drugs were not good for business, NBC had to put on a show. It was long before tabloid journalism became the norm, back when heroes were still somewhat protected. They blamed the Canadian for screwing up the great reputation of track and field, celebrated Carl Lewis's gold, and now they had another American who would politely and quietly step up to claim third place. Show biz.

Reporter Jim Gray was sent to the Athlete's Village to do a live shot. It was already close to ninety degrees at about 10 a.m. in Seoul. That's 9 p.m. eastern time at home. He and I were set up outside, in full sun, sitting in front of a couple of potted palms, waiting for our cue. We didn't talk until the cameras were on. Jim was sweating in his official NBC jacket and tie. I was sweating too, in jeans and a polo shirt. I didn't complain, but I certainly noticed that I was never treated like Carl Lewis.

When Carl Lewis was on television during these Games, he was in the air-conditioned studio, decked out in his nice leather jacket, not sweating, with Bryant Gumbel, who was also not sweating. By this time in my life I had already been a world record holder and an Olympic gold medalist and I had never even met Bryant Gumbel. I still haven't.

Below is the transcript of the interview that aired that night between two sweaty guys not saying much about anything, which was my fault.

Jim: Calvin, what's your reaction? Are you happy? Are you sad your event has been tainted?

Calvin: Well, there are some mixed emotions. I am very happy that now I will be getting the bronze medal and I'm somewhat sad that on that day I did run, I was not able to stand on the podium and get the respect as one of the top sprinters. That is what I feel that I should have gotten that day. It's just one of those things. I'm just glad that things have been cleared up now.

Jim: Had you suspected Ben?

Calvin: Well, um, I have suspected a number of athletes that may have been on drugs. As far as proving any athletes are on drugs, I can't do that, but, um, I think, you know, as far as feeling that there are some athletes on drugs, yes, I have felt that way.

Jim: Do you suspect that any of those above you are using drugs?

Calvin: Well, it's just at different events in general that I feel there are a number of athletes on drugs.

Jim: What does this do to you now? You get the bronze in somewhat of a tainted event and it kind of changes the complexion of the entire situation. Do you feel as though your event now is always going to be looked at as suspect by the public?

Calvin: Well, I don't think that it's going to always be looked at that way because I think this is a good example that will be set forth that will prevent more athletes from taking steroids. Now that they know they will be punished and will be caught if they decide to take drugs. So I think it will clear up the sport and hopefully it'll become a better sport in the sense that it'll be a clean sport.

What I should have said was that I deserved the gold and Robson Da Silva (Brazil), who also ran clean, deserved the silver medal. The druggies could fight over the bronze for all I cared.

Jim Gray was actually four years too late in his assessment of my "tainted event." It was my gold medal from the 1984 Olympics that I consider tainted. In my educated-with-inside-access opinion, Carl Lewis's performance was enhanced when he ran the anchor leg for our world record in the 4 x 100 meter relay at the Games of the XXIII Olympiad in Los Angeles. No, I can't prove it. But in my heart and in my mind, he tainted my 1984 gold medal achievement and I'll always remember the guilt I felt as if it happened yesterday. He didn't seem to care how his behavior reflected on our team and neither did the United States Olympic Committee (USOC), in my opinion, as long as we won.

In that interview out in the hot sun in Seoul, I did what the USOC required of me and didn't add fuel to the fire. I knew the scandal in 1988 was bigger than one disgraced Canadian sprinter on steroids. "It'll become a better sport," I told Jim Gray, and myself. Maybe I really did have a sliver of hope that things would change. I don't remember. When Jim and I parted ways, the show went back to the air-conditioned studio with a nice, dry Bryant Gumbel wrapping up a "sad and disappointing day" for the home audience.

NBC won a couple of Emmy Awards for their Olympic telecast from Seoul, despite that interview with me. I'm sorry I couldn't give Jim the rest of the story. So many Olympic athletes were only world-class-competitive with an edge, and that edge was cheating. I knew Ben was just the tip of the iceberg.

I often wondered if NBC set up Jim for that interview the same way I was prepped. The network surely had a lot to lose if a whole bunch of athletes were outed as cheaters.

Before the interview, I was advised, actually warned, by Coach Rogers. He reminded me that the USOC didn't want me to say anything negative about specific individuals, drugs, or those who condone the use of drugs. That meant coaches, among others. Did NBC expect the same from Jim Gray? I hoped not, but I couldn't be sure. I couldn't tell from his demeanor at the interview.

During the process of working on this book, I was happy to find out the network did not interfere with the reporting. Jim Gray says that producer Michael Weisman told him to "go get the story." He tried. He asked the right questions. I had the story, but said nothing. The USOC had another medal winner, and a team player, in Seoul.

Russ Rogers was in a delicate position. I could appreciate that. I considered him a friend. I still do. He did not condone the use of drugs and was an obvious favorite of those of us who ran clean. He had to act like a buffer among three groups: the clean runners, the dopers and the USOC. Oh, and he also had to put a winning team on the track. I know it drove him crazy to have to keep secrets. He knew he couldn't clean up the sport when so many coaches were handing out drugs that the track and field organizations didn't want to know about.

Coach Rogers has said many times since that race in '88, "Calvin and Robson da Silva were the only clean runners in that 100 meter race. Everybody knew that." And by everybody, he means all the people inside track and field. The man has coached for almost fifty years and he knows what he's talking about.

The 1988 Olympic medal from Seoul.

On the front, the goddess of victory holds a palm in her left hand and a crown in her right.

On the reverse side is the dove holding a laurel branch. Above it is the Olympic rings logo and an ancient Korean Taegeuk symbol which is also on the Korean flag.

Little did I know that a spot on team USA would lead to so many sports hall of fame ceremonies.

(courtesy John Elliott *Studio*)

2

Quiet Calvin

Most people will tell you how quiet I am. That's the impression I give. (Although people I work with now will tell you differently.) I never meant to be quiet. I just like to listen. You can learn a lot by listening.

My quietness was a double-edged sword when I ran on the U.S. team. On one hand, not talking about the doping going on behind the scenes allowed me to play in the big leagues. On the other, not speaking up about what was going on, made me a reluctant participant in the cover-up.

Running was my way out of Mississippi. Running was my way of going to college and making a living. I became successful in an organization that did some things I didn't agree with. I was no different than many other hard-working Americans. I quietly did my job despite not liking my boss.

Several years before I was born, there was another quiet Calvin. He was a deaf mute who lived in our neighborhood. He would come around the house to visit my mother. It might have had something to do with her baking. There was nothing wrong with his sense of smell or taste. She said the two of them communicated quite well with their own system of hand signals, smiles, and nods and they had fine visits. Not only did mother like Calvin, she liked his name and that's how it was passed on to me. Mother said the original Calvin was very proud when he learned the name of her new baby.

For a while though, mother came to regret naming me after that Calvin. She thought she had saddled me with the curse of silence because I didn't talk until I was nearly five years old. I don't remember that it was a problem for me.

My friend Bruce Cabot and I were both late bloomers as far as talking was concerned. At three and four years old, we were the quietest toddlers in the neighborhood. When one of us wanted to answer a question with a no, we'd just shrug our shoulders. If we needed to say yes, we smiled, big and wide.

The only word we were ever overheard to say was "go," and that was during the *big* races we held. All the other kids knew us as the zookeepers. We caught rabbits, squirrels, armadillos, you name it. We had little pens for them so we could keep them captive. Then we'd take them out, put them side by side and yell, "Go, go, go!" Of course the animals would go wherever they wanted. But at least our mothers knew we could talk. I guess we just didn't have anything else to say.

When the county worker came to register me for Head Start, my mother didn't think I was ready. Head Start is a pre-kindergarten for families of little means. I think everyone in my hometown of Bolton, Mississippi qualified for it. Mother told the woman I didn't talk and that's why she didn't want me to go. However, the lady said, "Let's try it. He'll be fine."

Mother wasn't so sure. She took me there herself, at first. Then one day, she asked me if I wanted to take the bus. My smile was big and wide. She knew what that meant.

I became more outgoing during that year of Head Start. One of the things I liked best about school was singing all those little-kid songs. I don't actually remember this, but my sisters say that once I learned them, I kept singing them. All the time. It got to the point where the other kids who used to try to get me to talk were now begging, "Mom, please shut him up."

When I got famous for my running, I wasn't much of a talker either. Coach Rogers used to say, "Calvin is quiet, but he's loud on the track." I trained so hard that I felt I was supposed to win. I didn't feel the need to tell people how fast I ran. They could see it.

Even as a young kid, I remember I had a master plan to work hard in school and do everything I could to live a good life. When running became my special talent, I knew I had a choice to brag or not to brag. If I had chosen to showboat, my career would have taken a different turn. I would have been sought after by the media and been expected to show my face here and there for publicity. I would have ended up on more magazine covers and gotten more endorsements. But that's not my way. The publicity would have been fine, but I couldn't distance myself from other people. That's not me. I didn't mind signing autographs and I liked meeting people from all over the world. In fact, I loved it. I wanted to be accessible. The fans enjoyed the sport and I enjoyed the fans, especially the kids.

My sister Angie says if she had known about the business end of track back then, she would have made me talk more and she would have marketed me, but I didn't think that way. I wanted to show young athletes you didn't have to do that. You could still achieve your goals, set world records, and even be an Olympic champion without putting other people down or raising yourself up by bragging.

My upbringing, family and church, helped me not to showboat. Can you imagine how quickly I would have been put in my place by all my brothers and sisters, not to mention my mom and her handy broom? We were brought up to understand that God has given us our gifts. I had to honor that.

After I won a gold medal in the 4 x 100 meter relay at the 1984 Olympics, I visited many schools to encourage kids to be goal-driven. I didn't bad-mouth anyone in the process. The children often asked about the high profile athletes, those who obviously were doping and promoting themselves. I said, "That is their way. That works for them. It doesn't take all that to be successful." I hoped those kids would find their own path.

There were other runners out there spreading the same message. Harvey Glance (Auburn University) and Mel Lattany (University of Georgia) are well-grounded people. They could inspire young people with the way they carried themselves on and off the track.

Guys like us, we had quiet attitude. We didn't get the magazine covers, but we also didn't get crooked teeth from injecting human growth hormone (which, by the way, only came from the pituitary glands of cadavers in the early '80s). We knew the dopers were going to do what they do. They put a lot of time and energy into playing superstars in public, while keeping all those secrets.

With me, what you saw was what you got. Quiet worked for me. My job was running. I was doing it well, having fun, and I was getting paid. I didn't need any more than that. Mom's old friend Calvin passed away many years ago, but I'd like to think he'd still be proud that I have his name.

This is one of the few pictures I have of my dad.

It was nice having a childhood in a rural town like Bolton. We got to use our imaginations. I think that dreaming of bigger places actually helped a lot of us get out and see the world.

(courtesy Jeff DeHayes)

Downtown Bolton today. More modern, but not any
bigger than the Bolton I left.
(courtesy www.LegendsOfAmerica.com)

3

Death and Life in
Bolton, Mississippi

I was just five years old when my father, Emmanuel Smith, died from hypertension. I don't remember much about him. Mother says he never heard me talk. "Not one word," she says. He was only 35 years old and he died the day before my mother's 32nd birthday. I learned the details much later.

Dad worked for the City of Jackson Waterworks Department, fixing water pipe leaks. He worked around our house too. He helped mother with the laundry. She did the washing on her scrub board and he hung the clothes outside to dry. He also helped get the little kids dressed for church. The boys had Sunday suits and the girls had nice dresses. And since seeing that our meat didn't come from the supermarket, Dad was our butcher. He was also our barber. We boys were forever grateful that he carefully observed the difference.

Dad was tall and thin and he never complained about being sick. In those days, in small-town Mississippi, no one went to a doctor unless they absolutely had no choice. Obviously, he waited too long to get checked for his high blood pressure. When mother took him to Dr. Reynolds in Clinton, the next town over, the doctor took her aside and told her that her husband was "mighty sick." He died a week later.

During that last week of his life, dad talked about dying and tried to help prepare mother to take care of the whole lot of us by herself. We already had chickens and pigs for food, and now he wanted us to get a cow for milk. Neither he nor mother wanted to accept welfare and they never did.

It was a very hot night when dad died. Mississippi hot, before anyone in Bolton had air-conditioning. Dad was in bed, but mom was on the couch with baby Angie. She said he came into the living room and kind of moaned. She asked him if he was too hot to sleep. He didn't answer. He just slumped to the floor. Mom called Sonny, the oldest, to come help and she ran down the street to get her parents. Almost all of mother's extended family lived on our street. That turned out to be a real blessing.

I was at my grandparents' house that night. I remember being on their front porch the next morning and someone came out and said "They're taking your dad away." I looked down the street and saw them putting a stretcher into a big black car, which I later learned was a hearse. I don't remember any more than that.

Mother needed to be sedated for three days. She says, "Every time I woke up, they'd give me another pill to knock me out." It was understandable. She was a widow with eight children. (Dad also had two older children, Jimmy and Dottie. They lived with their mother. Dottie passed away a couple of years ago.)

Of mother's brood, Larry (Sonny), the oldest, was thirteen when father died. Emmanuel Jr. (Dunny) was twelve. Belinda (Linda) was eleven. Allen (Dee) was ten. Samuel (Mane) was nine. Next was me at five and I never got a nickname. Luretha (Candy) was four and baby Angela (Angie) was just a year old. Mother truly had her hands full.

The funeral was held one week later and mother didn't recover for what she says was "quite a while." The older children helped take care of the younger ones. And our grandparents and other family members made sure our lives went on as smoothly as possible.

After mother recovered, a county worker came by and told her she qualified for assistance, but she already had dad's social security check and our little farm. Not wanting to accept charity, she started working herself. She became a housekeeper for some families in Clinton and she continued working for forty-one years. I know she was loved and appreciated by everyone she worked for. Even in her retirement, she continues to get very generous gifts every Christmas from those folks.

We lived in the Mt. Olive section of Bolton, Mississippi, a small town full of hard-working African American families. There was one store, owned by the Brown family, and that's where everyone went to hang out. It was near the church, the playground, and the community center. That was all there was to Bolton. I have no idea how many people lived there when I was a kid, but fifty years later, the population is still less than six hundred.

There was nothing multi-cultural about Bolton either. No Jewish deli or Irish pub or Italian Pizzeria. To even see a white person, you had to travel eight miles west on Interstate 20 to Clinton. And even though that's where the Bolton families sent their kids to the public schools, the white folks in Clinton sent their kids to private schools.

Funny thing though, every year there were a few white kids who started the school year with us. I guess they were new in town. They'd be there for about a month and then they would disappear. They probably transferred to private schools or moved away, but nobody talked about it and I never asked. It happened every year, so it became the norm.

We had both black and white teachers. We were used to that. To us, they were just teachers. It didn't matter what color they were.

Our doctor was white. Dr. Reynolds had an office in Clinton with two doors leading to two separate waiting rooms, one for whites and one for us. That's just how it was back then and nobody in my world made a big deal about it in front of the children. I didn't give any thought to what was separate, or if it was equal. I also never felt that I lacked anything.

By the time I was born on January 8, 1961, Mississippi already had a long track record of being the poorest state in the nation. Even today, that hasn't changed. And racism is a big part of our history.

James Meredith single-handedly desegregated the University of Mississippi, under tremendous protest, in 1962. Civil rights leader Medgar Evers was gunned down outside his home in Jackson in 1963, just hours after President Kennedy announced his proposal for the Civil Rights Act. Violence during the Freedom Summer of 1964 happened all over the state. There were lynchings and cover-ups and Ku Klux Klan rallies.

It was all around me. I thank God it was only around me and I was insulated. We were in a rural area and this was long before the internet and cable television. I saw people in Bolton work, play, worship and raise families. The adults did a terrific job of sheltering us. I have only happy memories of my childhood.

After the Civil Rights Act of 1964 was supposed to

put an end to discrimination, my father's family in California wanted to bring us out there. Mother and dad didn't even consider it. They knew they were providing a good home for us and they probably hoped the law would make a difference in Mississippi too, despite all they knew about how things worked in the Deep South. California, even with the new federal law, was a mystery to them.

As I grew older, I was exposed to the shameful reputation of my home state, first by hearing people talk. Then eventually, television. We turned the channel from sitcoms to the news and watched in disbelief at what was happening just 20 miles west, in Jackson. Firehoses, bricks and lead pipes were being used on black people right in the center of our capital city. Suddenly I realized I was not like Beaver Cleaver or Opie Taylor and I didn't live in Mayberry.

Seeing the horror of racism in my own state was life-changing. All at once I had to acknowledge the absence of simple human rights and freedoms for people like me. I finally had my eyes opened to segregation. We were separate, but not nearly as equal. The rest of the country looked upon Mississippi as the worst state a black person could live in, and now, so did I. Coincidentally, I also felt the need to get away from the Smith family home on Mt. Olive Road.

My brother Allen, we call him Dee, is five years older than I am and he was the one kid in the family who caused my mother the most trouble. With eight kids to raise on her own, her life was not easy. Seven of us felt a responsibility not to overload her with problems. And then there was Dee. He was *The Problem Child*.

Dee was the spitting image of our dad and he took that to heart, forecasting an early death for himself too. So, in order to test his theory, he became a daredevil by drinking a lot and driving a little. That is, he got drunk and then drove off bridges or into trees. He survived more car wrecks than I ever thought was possible. I can still see the pain on my mother's face every time she learned of a new crash. She kept saying, "This boy's just runnin' me crazy." And she was right. I needed to get away from seeing her hurt more than I needed to get away from his behavior. I could watch him crash, but I couldn't stand watching her worry.

Through witnessing Dee's behavior, I developed a great sense of right and wrong. With the guidance of my family, teachers and church, I was determined to be the anti-Dee. That goal probably helped me to stay focused, not only on running, but on succeeding in every area of my life.

As for Dee, he is now what mother calls, "the ideal child." Allen 'Dee' Smith finally grew up, got married and he has three children. Seems a doctor got through to him somewhere along the way and convinced him it was the drinking that would kill him, not the resemblance to our father. So he stopped drinking, which also made him stop acting like an idiot. At mother's eightieth birthday party, she reminisced about how bad he was and how he made the big turn to get on the right track before it was too late and killed *her.*

I got mother's attention in a more positive way. My first real success came in church. I excelled on the small stage at Mount Olive Baptist Church, where they regularly held public speaking contests for the children. The prize was that you would go on to represent your church in a bigger contest with other churches. We practiced poems and short speeches in Sunday school and, although I was considered one of the quiet kids, I found my voice when I was up there in front of the class. I was good at it, and just knowing that, gave me the confidence to get up in front of any audience. Thankfully, that has never left me because, as an Olympic gold medalist, I have had plenty of opportunity to address large groups.

When we weren't at school or church, we were

outside playing. This was the 1960s and '70s. No one knew what a couch potato was yet. We ran everywhere. We challenged each other to feats of strength and speed and it was fun to win. Kids used to come around from other neighborhoods to race. I was always the one they wanted to beat. I'd run against them, win, and call it a day. I don't recall ever losing.

I stood out in school because of my speed. In physical education class, all the boys wanted to play football. I didn't particularly care about football, but I liked to run, and that's what I did when they gave me the ball. That's all it took. They gave me the ball and I would run like the wind. I knew I had exceptional speed and now they knew I had it. No one could catch me. They just watched me run.

That's how it all started, or so I thought, before I began writing this book. But it actually started when my friend Bruce Cabot and I were little.

Bruce and I usually spent our non-school time at the playground out by the church, well over a mile away from our neighborhood. We left the house after breakfast, maybe went home for lunch if we didn't take a snack with us, and then came home at sundown. When you're little, you usually don't notice sundown until it's too late. Bruce and I stayed out as long as we could, so we often had to go home in the dark. In our minds, running down those dirt roads at night was a race against The Boogey Man.

We ran down one road and over a bridge together until we got to the big tree with the Spanish moss hanging down. Although grand and beautiful in the daylight, Bruce and I were sure it sheltered wicked demons in the dark. We named it "The Scary Ghost Tree." Once we reached that trcc, wc had to go our separate ways. I ran fast out of fear. That's really how it all started. "The Scary Ghost Tree" made me realize the importance of a having a final kick too. I had to save a little something in the run for my life, just in case The

Boogey Man jumped out at me on the last stretch of my way home.

There were plenty of times I had to be quicker than my seven siblings too, like when the pecans were ready to pick off the trees on our property. That was a matter of money. If you were able to pick the most pecans, you were able to sell the most pecans. As I grew older, I grew richer.

My sister Angie is four years younger than I am and just as competitive. We often raced from the house to the big plum tree about a hundred yards away. I always won. So as time went on, I had to give her an advantage to fuel her false hope that she might beat me.

One day I told her she could use her bike and I'd just run on foot, as usual. She was excited. But I was too confident. I made her nervous. She got anxious and pedaled so fast that she lost control of her bike and crashed. The chain broke off the bike and cut a deep gash in her leg. At first, I just kept running. But when I looked back, she was on the ground, crying. So I gave up the win, pulled the chain out of her leg and went to the doctor with her and mother. She needed fourteen stitches. I think we stopped racing each other after that, but we didn't stop competing.

Everyone loved mother's homemade pies. She baked every week and, except for the adult children who had left home, the rest of the crew had unwritten rules about the goods. One of them was "calling it." If there was one piece of pie left and you "called it," it was yours. No question about it. Well there was one time (truth be told, maybe more) that I wanted that last piece of pecan pie, but Angie "called it." We both held onto the plate pulling it between us, the pie getting all thrown about and falling, crumb by crumb, off the plate. Neither of us would let go. Mom came in on the ruckus in the kitchen and the first thing she did was pick up her broom. Before she swung it, she just watched. I guess she saw the humor in the whole situation and, as I ate whatever pie was left on the plate while Angie was still calling it, mom put down the broom and said, "Y'all just kill each other. I don't care." She had six other kids. I guess she figured the two of us were expendable if we couldn't behave.

Mother might have just been tired of all the nonsense by then. Angie, Candy and I were the three youngest and it's like we were the second family. The older kids weren't around much, except at night to sleep. I do remember three to a bed at one point. But the boys left home by age seventeen or eighteen and mother was still raising the three of us. I don't think we were even in high school by the time of the pie incident.

Now that I have two kids of my own, I realize how strong and resilient my mother was and always has been. After dad's death, nothing broke her. How she raised eight successful people who started out as knuckleheads is truly amazing.

The head of our family, Mother is beautiful inside and out.

Mother with seven of her eight children. That's me in white, front left.

That's Angie on the left and her husband Geno Lee on the right. Their youngest daughter, Bella, and oldest, Tori, are on either side of Deuce McAllister, running back for the New Orleans Saints, and the Ole Miss Rebels. Deuce and I were inducted into the Mississippi Sports Hall of Fame on the same night in 2014.

(courtesy John Elliott *Studio*)

4

Sumner Hill High School

Sumner Hill High School was a combination of middle school and high school. We had grades seven through twelve in the same building and we called all of it Sumner Hill High School.

Roger Norman, my physical education teacher, was also the track coach at Sumner Hill. His main job was teaching but his first love was baseball. He used to play. I'm not sure how far he got with it, but he never stopped talking about how much he loved his playing days. We didn't have a baseball team at our school. We didn't even have a baseball field.

Mr. Norman took the track coaching position because no one else wanted it. He knew next to nothing about track and neither did I, so we made a good pair. We were schooled in track together, but not for a while.

When he got me to come out for the team in eighth grade, it didn't stick. Although I loved to run, I didn't love the process of actually becoming a runner who could compete in events as part of a team. It was too much work.

I had never practiced running before. I just ran. And I was upset to discover that too much of this practicing led to an awful lot of pain. I didn't realize, or want to accept, the muscle aches that would come from the hard work of being part of a track team. It was the first time I got involved in an organized sport and I didn't know what I was getting into. So I quit. I didn't need that. I knew I could run faster than most people, but the practice required for being on the team was a killer.

The school was in Clinton and we lived in Bolton, so I didn't even watch the track team that year because transportation was an issue. I went to some football and basketball games with friends, when I could get a ride, but not one track meet. I kept thinking about it though. They didn't have much of a team and they could have used me.

By the next season, I had matured a little and I was ready. I had a better understanding about practice and I came to the great realization that the muscle aches would eventually go away, especially after a long soak in warm water and Epsom salts. It was a small price to pay for the feeling of accomplishment I got from crossing the finish line first.

Coach Norman was better the next year too. He told us that he had read up on the events in track and field and was going to do the best he could to help us compete. So with a book-smart coach and a bunch of kids who wanted to win something, anything, we began again. We put our trust in Coach Norman because we liked and respected him. But honestly, it's not like we had a line of people fighting to coach us.

There was another kid on the team, Lawrence Thomas, who was a good sprinter too, and we pushed each other in practice. The competition made both of us better than either one of us would have been alone. We worked hard every day just to beat each other and that helped us beat everyone else. Fortunately for me, it also helped me beat Lawrence in most of the meets. I handled the competition better than he did. I won the state meet in the 200 meters all four years and took the 100 meters in three out of four years.

Lawrence went on to Mississippi State and had a pretty good career there. I almost went there too, because we talked about running together. But I changed my mind at the last minute and decided to stick to my goal of leaving Mississippi, since the opportunity had presented itself. Lawrence and I remained friends and competitors.

I liked high school. I was in the higher academic classes, but I had friends in all the typical school groups: nerds, jocks, drama and chorus kids. I liked everyone, but I didn't tolerate the bullies. I didn't fight them, I just kept quiet and threw them a mean look. That's all it took. The kids said I had a great mean look.

Thanks to my success on the track, I was pretty popular by my senior year, so I decided to run for Mr. Sumner Hill. If I won, I wouldn't need a hall pass for the whole year and I'd get to go to all the school events for free. I'd also recharge a family tradition. One of my aunts had been Miss Sumner Hill.

I ran against one of my best friends, Major McIntyre. He was popular too, but he didn't know how to play to an audience like the veteran public speaker I was. I had all that church experience. At the start of the election season, each of us had to address the entire senior class to tell them why we wanted to be Mr. Sumner Hill.

Major went first. He got up and talked about

himself like any kid would, but there was nothing memorable about his speech. He finished to polite applause.

Then I got up to the podium and smiled. I looked around the audience. After that moment of silence I simply said, "Look at me." I paused again, a nice long pause. I smiled confidently and let 'em look. They had the time to consider me from what they already knew. Then I pointed to them and said, "You should vote for me as Mr. Sumner Hill." Another pause. It was a stunning moment, if I do say so myself. The applause began and my title was in the bag. Of course I still made posters and went out of my way to talk to as many people as I could before the election. But I think my minute on stage was the difference. And I hardly said anything, as usual.

Sidney Poitier might have had something to do with my popularity at the time too. I had just come off a fine run of playing Walter Lee Younger in our school production of *A Raisin in the Sun*, my junior year. I'm not sure what got into me, but that's the part I auditioned for and I got it. Those who thought I was quiet before this, got to see just how outgoing I could be.

Our drama teacher, Mr. Luby, made class so much fun. I loved acting class. We had emotions on that stage and we weren't shy about letting them out.

I remember that every performance of *A Raisin in the Sun* played to standing ovations. That's my story and I'm sticking to it. Even the one where I took Walter and Momma off script. I messed up my lines one night. A girl named Corinne was playing Momma and she picked up on it right away. Instead of stopping me, she went off script too and we just kept talking until I got back on track. The audience didn't know the difference and Mr. Luby was proud of us for not breaking character.

I was officially the best athlete from the state of

Mississippi in 1979. All of athletes, from each state, were invited to Chicago for a big awards presentation where we each got a large trophy shaped like the number one.

I was proud to represent Mississippi and I knew this was just the beginning. I was on the road to chasing my dreams of winning Olympic medals and setting world records like my heroes, Jesse Owens and Jim Hines. In fact, just 4 years after this Chicago ceremony, I would go on to break Jim Hines' 100 meter world record of 9.95 which he set at the 1968 Olympics. That was a special accomplishment for me. It made me feel like I had arrived.

During the track season of my senior year in high school, Coach Norman and I traveled around the country to as many big high school meets as we could. We went to the Golden West Meet in Sacramento and some other huge event in the Chicago area. We needed an audience of college track coaches so that I could get recruited. That season was all about getting an athletic scholarship and it worked out well. I made a name for myself and the schools came after me.

Of course the Mississippi schools wanted me. There's nothing like home-grown talent to put some fire into your fan base. But I wasn't interested in them. Like I said earlier, I learned that Mississippi wasn't the place for a young black man and I wanted to get far away from my brother Dee.

There was a long line of coaches waiting to talk to mother about my future. My high school principal had already warned her about how they would likely try to bribe her with money to influence me. The SEC (Southeastern Conference) has a scandalous history and, geographically, the SEC practically encircles Bolton, Mississippi. But their infractions were mostly in football and this was track. Mother didn't get offered nearly enough money to sway her, so the decision was mine alone.

My sister Linda was the only family member to have gone to college at this point. She went to Jackson State, close to home, and got her degree to be a physical education teacher.

UCLA was at the top of my list of schools. I knew they had a first class track program. Jim Bush was the coach and he had already led them to five NCAA Championships.

My cousin Benny, also a runner, was on the team at UCLA. Benny was one of the Californians on my father's side of the family. I hardly knew him, but I wanted to see UCLA and the school invited me for a visit. The campus was beautiful and it was far away from Mississippi. Ultimately, that was the problem. It was too far away. I knew I wouldn't have the money to make the trip home when I needed to. So, just like that, my dream moved about two thousand miles back east.

I visited Mississippi State, Ole Miss, Mississippi Valley State and Alabama. Wayne Williams was the Alabama coach who recruited me. Back then, the NCAA didn't put any limits on phone calls to recruits. In addition to coming to my big meets, Coach Williams called me several times a week, sometimes twice a day. He didn't pressure me. We just talked about stuff. He got me thinking about what I wanted out of college. I later found out he was working from some magazine article he found, titled *The Top 20 Ways to Recruit*. The bottom line is that he talked about all aspects of the school and college life, not just the track team. That made me feel comfortable, like I could call the place home. Besides, I knew Alabama had recruited very good athletes at this time and I thought the track team had the potential to do well immediately.

It turned out I was right. We won the Southeastern Conference Championship in my freshman year. I liked all the coaches and the campus, and I loved the accommodations they provided for the track team. It was first class, just like UCLA, but still driving distance from Bolton. After careful consideration, I signed late, in July or August.

My high school track coach, Roger Norman,
and one of many track-themed birthday
cakes.

Here I am with my award for being the best athlete in Mississippi in 1979.

Coach Wayne Williams recruited me for the team at
Alabama and he's been with me ever since. A true
friend.

Mississippi has produced many of our country's elite athletes, so when I saw this storefront in (of all places) Nice, France, I just had to stop and get my picture taken.

5

Roll Tide

If you're not from Mississippi, I realize that my so-called escape to Alabama doesn't look like much of a trek, but it was to me. It was a world away from my troubled brother, albeit a similar world. Once again, my environment was anything but multi-cultural, but now it was full of mostly white American students. Being in the minority and away from friends and family was hard. It also left me open to what was really going on in the South. The University of Alabama was where I first came face-to-face with racism.

I wanted to study computer science in the School of Business. I was in the higher level classes at Sumner Hill and I thought I was as prepared as any incoming college freshman. Wrong. The separate-but-not-equal reality of my high school education smacked me in the face in math class. I struggled to keep up and I was staying up all night trying to do my assignments. Thank goodness I was smart enough to know that if I spent all my time on math, I wouldn't have the energy to run track. So I quickly switched my major to public relations. Of course, communication is a large part of public relations, so I had to take a lot of English and writing courses. After all the experience I got with my church speeches, I knew I could handle those. Wrong again. Well, sort of.

A white lady professor in my first college English class greeted me with, "You might as well drop my class now because you're not going to pass it." Not the welcome I was expecting for a star track athlete who was recruited to come here. She obviously didn't know who I was. I didn't know her either, but I was willing to give her a chance. I stayed long enough to hand in one assignment. When she handed it back to me the next day, it looked like she had cut an artery. I had never seen so much red ink on a simple composition. I didn't darken her doorway again. Pun intended. And until now, I have never said a word about it.

I thought about what my high school guidance counselor had said about going to white schools. He said that although it would be different, we were just as good as any other student. However, we might have to work harder to prove ourselves. I was willing to do that, but not in that woman's class. With other professors, I was treated like every other student and I did fine.

My freshman year at Alabama was really the first time I ever had professional track coaches. Coach Norman's book smarts got me this far, but I soon realized I had a lot to learn. Coach Williams said I had all the raw talent I needed, but he intended to make me a better runner through the program they had developed. We began in the fall. I was open to all of it, except for the part that took me into the weight room.

We had a strength coach who set up a series of exercises for each of us. Squats, bench presses, lifting and more. It was all new to me and I was embarrassed that I didn't know my way around the equipment. I watched and I tried, but on most days I just made an appearance and then left because I felt intimidated. It wasn't Coach Williams' way to get on me for skipping out. He mentioned it, but left it up to me. I stayed on campus and went to summer school that first year. Without the rest of the team around to watch me, I learned to use that weight room. And I built up a lot of muscle on my 150 lb. frame, if I do say so myself.

Coach Williams also got me to straighten up a little. He said my big Afro tilted too much to the left and back. So with drills and techniques to make me better mechanically, and a shorter haircut, he corrected my form so that I only tilted slightly to the left and back. That really worked out well for me.

During my time at Alabama, and at the World Championships, and later the Olympics, Coach Williams, and the other coaches I had, considered me to be the best turn runner in the world because of that little lean. That's why I always ran the third leg of the 4 x 100 meter relay. I was fastest through the turn. The top guy doesn't have to run the anchor leg in a relay, despite what you might hear from Carl Lewis.

My Alabama teammate Emmit King, who ran the first leg on our world record relay team in 1983, anchored the relay when we were still in school. He was so great on the hand-off, really smooth. He also ran the 100 meters. He came to Alabama from a junior college and I was happy to have him on the team. He was outgoing and talkative and he didn't hesitate to tell everyone about his amazing speed. He was downright entertaining. Even when he lost a race, he'd start trash-talking for the next event right after he crossed the finish line. He beat me a lot when we were in school and early in the season when we went pro. That's when I was working to get better. But after Alabama, by the middle of the pro season, I always shut him up. I could wave at him as I passed by. That's how I remember it.

By the way, the other two runners on that 1983 world record team were Willie Gault (University of Tennessee) and Carl Lewis (University of Houston). You'll read more about Carl later. As for Willie and me, we got along very well. He did the hurdles and the relay. The only thing that kept him from being an Olympic champion was the 1980 boycott.

After the World Championships in Helsinki in 1983, Willie Gault had a gold medal and a world record, got drafted by the Chicago Bears, and eventually won a Super Bowl. He's in the Bears' Super Bowl Shuffle video and, after retiring from the NFL (National Football League), he dabbled in acting. He eventually came back to track and field, competing in the Masters Athletics events sanctioned by the USATF (USA Track & Field). The Southeastern Conference has certainly produced plenty of track talent.

Being a student athlete at Alabama had other perks besides the high-caliber competition in the SEC and that fine weight room.

I never once stayed in a dorm at Alabama. That was a big factor in winning me over on my recruitment visit. The athletes got to stay in apartments. Big, roomy apartments with bathrooms you didn't have to share with seven brothers and sisters. Of course, Paul 'Bear' Bryant's football team, they were the *chosen* ones. He was still coaching when I arrived. He retired after his 1982 season, my sophomore year.

Although the other teams on campus lived in the shadow of the illustrious football team, we didn't care because Coach Bryant shared the wealth at dinner time. We had breakfast and lunch at the same dorm, with the regular students each day. The food was typical cafeteria quality. But we got to have our dinner at Bryant Hall where the football team dined. All that wonderful food, and oh my, the steaks. I had never seen such steaks. They were tender, juicy and flavorful, unlike any steak I ever had before or since. They fed us like champions and that made us feel like champions. Dinner at Bryant Hall was a luxurious banquet every night. A feast. No wonder the Crimson Tide rolled over everyone else on that football field. They were full.

I must point out that even though the breakfast and lunch menu wasn't great at the local dorm, there were other benefits. It's where I met my beautiful wife, Melanie. One of the greatest things about her is she always understood why I wouldn't have dinner with her at school. Roll Tide.

Melanie and I during our wedding.

And here I am with Mother, my
other best girl, on that big day.

My time at Alabama was well spent. I left with a wife, an education, and a career that took me around the world.

This is the college man ready to step out onto the world stage.

6

Coaching a Winner

Running is not easy. Sure, almost everyone can do it, but not everyone can produce what appear to be super-human times with each subsequent event during the season.

Professional running is hard work. Full-time work. Your body is your instrument and you are the only one who can keep it finely tuned. That means you must maintain total control over what you put into it and what you get out of it. But even that takes a hit once in a while due to illness and injury.

It's unsettling for a runner to feel the effects of even the smallest aches, pains or allergies. They play havoc with your control. On the days you know your performance is questionable, you've got to have confidence that your training and self-discipline make you race-ready more often than not. On your good days, you can fly.

Fortunately for me, I've never had to think about food during my running years. I gave no regard to what I ate or when I ate. I've always had this lean body type. I was 5'10", 145 lbs. in high school. I ran in college at 5'10", 152 lbs. And as part of the U. S. team I was 5'10", 152 lbs. Even now, in my fifties, I'm 5'10", 152 lbs. and I can still eat anything I want without worrying about getting fat. Well, right now anyway. I still run almost every day. Maybe if I stopped running I'd pop a button or two.

When I started to run competitively, I tried to gain weight. I didn't get on any special program. I just ate more food. But I was training hard and burned it all off. I didn't gain a pound. The reason I wanted to gain weight was to help me to face the headwinds in those big stadiums in Europe. If I had more power, it might have been easier for me to run at those stadium events. But my body just doesn't work that way. Instead, my thin frame has to slice through the wind. I thought if I weighed more, I could push through a headwind with more muscle mass so the wind wouldn't blow me back as much. But I've never been able to test that theory. Really, not one pound.

Not having to think about my diet, I enjoyed a kind of freedom when it came to race-day preparation. Other runners had rituals with timing their hydration and nutrition. That gave them a lot to think about leading up to an event. Not me. I just showed up and ran. Full stomach or empty stomach, thirsty or not, it didn't matter.

My one exception was soda. I always cut down on soda during racing season. I love soda, but even when I was a kid, with my limited education in nutrition, I knew the sugar in soda was bad for me. So my rule was, no soda except on weekends. It wasn't until I got to college that I learned more about certain ingredients in foods and how they can affect the body.

I had been drinking coffee every morning since I

was in the fifth grade. Not for any reason other than I liked coffee and that's what we did in our house. Mornings were for coffee. I didn't think about it and I'm sure I had never even heard the word caffeine until I got to the University of Alabama. There I learned that the caffeine in my morning coffee was a stimulant and it was addictive. I didn't believe it.

I took pride in my lean, fast, runner's body and I had faith that my training program was all I needed to maintain it. This caffeine thing sounded crazy to me, but I couldn't let it go. The idea that something could exert control over my body, gnawed at me. So I conducted my own experiment and stopped drinking coffee, cold turkey. I was positive that there would be no consequences. Wrong. The headaches were awful. And since this was the only change I made to my so-called diet, I had to admit that my body was addicted to caffeine. It's the only time I have ever felt defeated. It made me angry. Nothing was going to beat me, certainly not coffee. I wanted to be back in control.

It took a while, but I weaned myself off caffeine by having coffee every other day, then skipping several days. I got to the point where I could enjoy a cup without having any headaches. I still don't think I needed to kick the habit, but I wanted to beat it and I did. Achieving self-control, that's a victory I savor.

I think that, to this day, I'm still the only self-coached Olympic athlete. It's not that I don't want any help. I've always had plenty of good people around me. But if you take responsibility for yourself, you have the power to shape your own future. I see great value in that. I felt I could manage my career far better than anyone else. I'm sure other people would tell you I was just stubborn. But I had the self-discipline to do it and more importantly, only I knew what my body was capable of. No one ever pushed me as hard as I pushed myself.

I sort of left my college coaches before I actually

left Alabama. It was nothing personal and I didn't make a big deal about it. I just used the format of the workouts I did in college and didn't worry about pleasing a coach.

Coaches have a tendency to ignore whomever is hurt in order to focus on the greater good of the team. I got hurt during the 1983 season and, all of a sudden, I felt ignored and expendable. It was then that I realized I was the only one who was fully invested in Calvin Smith.

Coaching myself didn't stop me from learning though. I charted all my workouts in order to view, on paper, how I was progressing. I could see my peaks and valleys and use this data to get ready at the right time. I was also open to advice, from both coaches and my peers.

(You can find a link to my daily workouts, leading up to various track meets, at the end of this book.)

Harvey Glance was a teammate of mine when we won the 4 x 100 meter relay in the 1987 World Championships in Rome. He was also one of the clean runners in U.S. Track and Field. He graduated from Auburn University with a degree in health and human performance. Isn't that a great line of study for a sprinter? I'm just one of the many runners thankful for Harvey's education and how he was always open to sharing what he learned. It was inevitable that he would become a great track and field coach, first as an assistant at Auburn and then as head coach at my alma mater, Alabama. I consider him a mentor. He was a good training partner too. We could motivate each other to work hard and practice so that those of us non-drug users could sometimes beat the drugged-up runners.

Although I did very well in my first World Championships in 1983 (first place in the 200 meters and second in the 100 meters, plus the world record in the relay), I was a more relaxed runner in my next World

Championships in Rome in 1987. Coach Richard Thompson, who had been coaching Harvey, schooled me on stride patterns. Multiply stride length by stride frequency and you get your speed. The only way you change that speed is to change one of those factors. Coach Thompson wanted me to have longer strides by getting my knees higher. That causes you to lengthen your stride. Then all you have to do is work on your speed.

So Coach Calvin Smith had a little bit of help from other coaches along the way and it was a good thing too, especially at the 1987 World Championships in Rome. I was hurt and all that coaching information in my head kept my mind off the pain.

My left leg, around the groin area, was giving me a lot of trouble. It was okay while I was running the straightaways, but I could feel pain once I hit the turns. There's more pressure on your legs in the turn. One of the other guys on the team started talking to me about visiting a chiropractor. I didn't actually know what a chiropractor did, but I remember thinking that the guy couldn't make it any worse. And since he wasn't a "real doctor," I knew I wasn't going to get any injections or pills. What could it hurt to let him look? It turned out to be one of the biggest mistakes I ever made.

Now remember, I was in Rome. But this wasn't any Italian chiropractor with fancy European gimmicks that I might have bought into, due to the language barrier. The U.S. team had its own chiropractor who traveled to the meets, just in case. The American "almost-doctor" said to me, "Let me straighten your leg out." I fully understood him and expected him to do just that. But he pulled and twisted. There was no straightening involved, and then the real pain began. Pain like I had never felt before. It was so bad, I think I started yelling at him in Italian. And he couldn't make it stop.

When I got to the track, the trainers worked on

my leg, trying to undo whatever the chiropractor had done. It wasn't helping. I ran the first round with teeth clenched. And every moment I sat, the trainers were with me, massaging and stretching. They were also using psychology, telling me that I could still run to win, if only from the anger I was feeling. I believed them. I channeled the pain and anger and I ran with the determination to win. In the preliminaries, I just put all the pain out of my mind for 20 seconds and made it to the finals of the 200-meter event.

I was in lane six or seven for the finals, not usually the most coveted spot, but I was happy because of the turns. It's a wider turn from the outside so there's less pressure on the legs. It was the longest 200 meters of my life, but I had enough left down the straightaway to get to the tape at 20.16 seconds, the same time as Gilles Queneherve of France. I won the gold by a fraction of a hundredth of a second. They had to look at the photo finish to determine the winner.

The trainers were waiting close to the finish line. I expected to be met with shouts of, "We knew you could do it!" Instead, they all 'fessed up and said, "We can't believe you actually did that." They admitted they were standing so close to the finish line because they thought they would have to carry me off the track.

When the 1987 season was over, I took it easy. I went to other events for the appearance fee, but I just jogged around the track. And I never, ever, went back to a chiropractor. I know people who go regularly and they say it works for them. Not me. Never again. I want my un-centered body to stay un-centered. It has served me well so far.

Coach Richard Thompson was instrumental in preparing me for the World Championships of 1987 and the 1988 Olympics.

Harvey Glance and me, enjoying the pre-race
sunshine and ceremony.

Lillie Leatherwood is another Alabama athlete who went on to Olympic gold in 1984. She currently makes her home in Tuscaloosa where she is a police officer.

7

"Amateur" Athletes

Back when I focused my attention on the Olympics, in the late 1970s through the '80s, I saw that the biggest competition for the Americans were the men and women from the Eastern Bloc countries. Not so much for the quality of any one particular athlete, they didn't have big sports stars on magazine covers like we did, but for the sheer quantity of athletes who were able to train full-time.

One glimpse of those teams and it was obvious that those countries were subsidizing their athletes. Their teams were packed with people who looked like they were ready to compete, a different kind of amateur from those of us in the United States. They were being paid to train, given housing, equipment, and stipends. When a government paycheck needed to be validated, they were even given jobs, in name only, of course. They didn't have time to work on anything but winning. I'll address their muscular bodies a bit later.

Amateurism, as we Americans know it, came to an end for most of the sports world in 1971. That's when the International Olympic Committee declared it was okay for athletes to receive compensation for training and competing. But even though what the Europeans had been doing for many years was now officially sanctioned by the IOC, the United States self-imposed a higher standard. Our country seemed to have a moral obligation to keep some truth in the word "amateur." It took seven more years for the United States to realize the Olympics were no longer a level playing field and real amateurs were not going to fare well against the pros.

In 1978, the Ted Stevens Amateur Sports Act became law, allowing athletes on the U.S. Olympic team to be compensated for their participation by way of financial awards, sponsorships and other types of payments. As of this writing, that piece of legislation is still not recognized by the National Collegiate Athletic Association (NCAA).

Many of our Olympic athletes are young enough to be in school. If they want to compete in college, the NCAA requires them to be honest-to-God amateurs, regardless of their Olympic dreams.

The NCAA Eligibility Center staff actually began certifying college athletes as *real* amateurs in the fall of 2007. Perhaps they didn't trust the colleges to do it themselves anymore. But hey, that's just my opinion. It's also my opinion that there are loopholes and backdoors and the NCAA looks the other way. Those brand new running shoes you see college athletes wearing don't just fall off the back of a truck, you know.

The current official loophole allows for "necessary expenses," so that students continue to maintain their amateur status without actual paychecks. But I know big money was out there in my day and I believe it's still out there today, regardless of the rules.

When I was at Alabama, the athletic shoe companies had representatives at all the NCAA track and field meets, looking for athletes who might be able to further their brand. They needed those competitors who could carry their label across the finish line first, on national television and in those huge track and field stadiums in Europe. Sometimes those stadiums held standing-room-only crowds of over sixty thousand fans. Track is as big in Europe as college football is here in America. A human billboard provided exactly what corporations needed to sell more shoes and sweats, and they were willing to pay for it. So in order to work around the NCAA rules of non-payment for student athletes, those companies set up trust funds and deferred-payment accounts.

My first and only sponsorship deal while I was in college was with Nike. They had a good reputation for supporting track and field. Their signature "swoosh" sign was introduced in 1972 at the U.S. Track and Field Olympic Trials in Eugene, Oregon. I was glad to wear their logo, and their rep made me an offer that included lots of athletic apparel. The money part of the deal was to be mine after I finished school. And keeping in mind the NCAA rules for amateur athletes, our agreement was a verbal one.

After I graduated, I eagerly anticipated receiving my paycheck. When it didn't arrive, I tracked down the rep and he said he had already given me the money. I politely suggested to him that he was surely mistaken. A kid from tiny, rural, Bolton, Mississippi, with seven siblings and a hard-working mother who were all relieved that I was on athletic scholarship, was not likely to forget a payment that would help with all my living expenses. After all, college was over and so was my scholarship. At this point I was kicking myself for that verbal agreement. Even a scrap of paper would have been better than nothing. My success took Nike to great heights in Europe. I had several first place finishes. They got more than their money's worth. I fulfilled my part of the deal and expected to be paid.

Well, the check took so long to arrive that I had plenty of time to get over my brand loyalty. I didn't trust the Nike rep anymore, and now that I no longer had to toe the line for the NCAA, I gave up the "swoosh" for Adidas.

Adidas is a German company that was started in 1924 by a couple of brothers working in their mother's laundry room, or so the story goes. Although they got many German runners to wear their shoes for Hitler's Olympics in 1936, they literally struck gold with U.S. sprinter Jesse Owens. The American was a clear favorite to do well in Berlin after his performance at the Olympic Trials.

One of the brothers, Adi Dassler, was a friend of German track coach, Jo Waitzer. Reports say he got Waitzer to give a few pairs of shoes to Owens. Running in them, Owens won four gold medals and put the company on the map.

Jesse Owens was a role model for me. He had done what sprinters only wish they could achieve. He was the one I strived to be like during my career. So, if Adidas shoes were good enough for Jesse, they were good enough for me. And this time I entered into a written contract with Adidas that left nothing to chance.

To those of us young men from rural areas and universities in the South, you can imagine how the world opened up to us when our track and field careers took us to faraway places. Agents took care of our travel plans and put together the schedule of our meets. We were happily doing our jobs while having all kinds of fun. It wasn't just the money, it was the adventure. Yes, we had an itinerary, and together, we were expected to follow it. It didn't matter to us that we didn't have a tour guide or a chaperone. We were 19 or 20 years old, traveling with a bunch of teammates in Europe, and we were fearless. And boys being boys, each one of us expected too much of the other guy. It's a wonder we got anywhere.

We didn't speak the languages. We didn't recognize most of the food. Yet we took it all in and had loads of laughs, often leaving a lasting impression of "those crazy American kids."

I remember one time we were on a train somewhere in Europe, going from one meet to another. No one around us spoke English and we were worried about where we were supposed to get off. Each of us relied on the others and nobody had a clue. As we pulled out of a station stop, one of the guys realized we were on the wrong train.

If you ever watched *I Love Lucy*, you probably know what's coming. It was exactly like the episode where she's on the train in Europe and keeps pulling the emergency brake rope because she thinks there's a criminal in the next compartment. That rope wasn't a Hollywood creation. There really was an emergency brake, operated by a rope, in many of the train cars in Europe in those days. Our group of college guys from Alabama, Georgia and Mississippi probably noticed the brake because of *I Love Lucy*. So, we knew exactly how to stop the train. Without hesitation, we pulled it. It was an abrupt stop, just like on television. If Fred and Ethel Mertz were eating in the dining car, they got covered with food again. We grabbed our gear and ran off the train as fast as we could. Remember, we were track stars. Nobody was going to catch us.

As I recall, we made it to the meet on time and learned a valuable lesson. We each took it upon ourselves to understand the itinerary and travel plans from that moment on. However, I must admit some of us still relied on the other guy for the details.

Back in the early '80s, all of those European hotels in quaint little towns surrounded by mountains, had actual keys to the rooms, not those key cards we have today. And I swear every one of those keys was big and silver. They all looked alike and there was no identification on them, except maybe a tag with your room number. When you're 19, and excited about being in a new town, and you have time to kill, you quickly put that key in your pocket and go out to explore the shops and cafes right after you check in. That's exactly what my roommate Mike Franks (Southern Illinois University) and I did when we arrived in Spain.

We had a great time, looking around for souvenirs and checking out the local eateries. After spending the whole afternoon walking around and taking in the sights, I said to him, "Hey Mike, it's getting late. We'd better go back to the hotel." He agreed and then it hit us, like a ton of bricks. We both looked at each other with a blank stare, yet full recognition of the problem at hand. We had been walking for a couple of hours and neither one of us remembered which direction we came from.

You see, when you run track, you run on an oval. A sprinter covers a few hundred meters, at the most. There are starting blocks and a finish line. You run away from the sound of the gun that starts the race and the track set-up practically points the way for you to go. It's foolproof, so a good sense of direction is not a requirement. I've never seen anybody run the wrong way on a track. At least not yet. My real life experience is a little different.

Somewhere in Spain, Mike and I were relying on each other to remember the name and address of our hotel. That turned out not to be the best plan. From the big silver keys in our pockets, all we could do was confirm our room number. Even if we saw a policeman, how could we ask him to take us to a place we couldn't name at an address we didn't know? That would have been embarrassing.

The only thing we knew for sure was that our hotel had brightly colored patio chairs on the second floor balcony. So we walked the village in kind of a circular pattern from our current starting point, looking up at the balconies. Eventually we found those chairs. That was rock bottom for me. I became a very responsible traveler after that. I'm even one of the few men who will stop and ask for directions when the route is not as clearly marked as the track.

Sometimes our most memorable travel stories had nothing to do with anything we did. We just happened to be at the right place at the wrong time. That's when you know God has a plan.

Authorities once kept our national junior track team stuck on the runway in Detroit for several hours because a bomb threat was discovered before take-off. They told us the threat said there was "a bomb on the plane." But they didn't let us get off. I kept wondering, if there was a bomb on the plane, why were we all just sitting there? I guess they had our trust. Thankfully, there was no bomb.

When planes are your way of commuting to work, I think it's best to trust in the Lord as well as the pilots. I know they both heard me one night on a puddle jumper in Italy. Those little planes shouldn't fly in bad weather. I was sitting next to Nat Page, a high jumper from the University of Missouri, now a coach at Georgia Tech. We hit major turbulence, worse than any roller coaster you can imagine. I'll never forget the look on his face. It said, "We're going to die." One of us might have yelled it out loud too. And then we prayed. Thankfully, it was not our time.

My worst flight ever, ended with a bang in Portland, Oregon. I was headed home to Tampa and one of the engines blew up just as we got off the ground. The plane came down on the runway with loud bang. I could see the smoke coming from the bad engine. The flight crew immediately opened the doors and threw out those inflatable chutes for us to slide down. Funny, but there was no chaos. Everybody was really quiet and moved out in an orderly fashion. No one was hurt, so we knew it could have been worse. A few hours later, all of us non-atheists boarded another plane. Like I told my family, "I'm not going to drive home all the way from Portland. That's over three thousand miles."

I built up a little nest egg, thanks to all that travel and those European adventures, and after college I didn't need to work at a normal job. I was grateful I had the education to get one, but I found I could make a six-figure salary running. I had product sponsors and track club sponsors and I was winning the bonus checks too. It couldn't have been better.

Travel had become a big part of my life because, even though there were sponsored meets going on in the United States, they weren't well-attended or covered by worldwide media, so they didn't pay well. I had to keep going to Europe to make the big money.

It was fine with me and I remember all of us American college track athletes were treated very well in Europe. They loved us and they are crazy about track and field. We grew a great fan base for the international contests that were still to come for many of us. To this day I'm recognized in Europe. Not so much here at home.

After we were married, Melanie almost always traveled with me, so it was like vacationing, except for the practice and the running. We did typical tourist things when I had down time. In Paris it was the Eiffel Tower. In Rome, the Coliseum. We saw grand churches and museums all over Europe. The travel was a nice perk to my career and I'm glad we got the chance to be globetrotters while we were young. When you first go to a famous place that you've only read about, it's exciting to see things come to life. Melanie loved the shopping too. She always seemed to find something new that would only become popular in the U.S. many months later.

Mother and the rest of the family back home in Mississippi loved it when we came home from a long trip. I brought back souvenirs from all around the world for my sisters and brothers. For my practical mother, I usually brought her some gifts, and helped her out financially.

Mom had her own share of notoriety in Bolton and Clinton. She represented the Mt. Olive Baptist Church at various meetings and, with eight children, plenty of folks knew her as so-and-so's mother too. But her fame also rose as I was getting publicity for winning races. She was "Mother of the Year" at our church while I was running professionally. By that time, even Angie was grown up, so it was more like an award for surviving eight kids. She loved it. It gave her a chance to make a speech and she was good at that.

Mother is proud of all her children, but with me, she could share something different with her friends, neighbors and even strangers. "My son Calvin is running in big stadiums all around the world and setting records and making a whole lot of money." That's what she would say when anyone just said, "Hello ma'am."

I kept telling her, "Mom, people don't want to hear all that." But she never stopped. She was so proud. It was all good.

That's me, the U.S. "amateur" in the white shirt, standing next to three non-American professionals. The man on the left is Atlee Mahorn of Canada, who ran at Cal Berkeley. The tall man is Linford Christie of Great Britain. On the right is Mark McKoy of Canada.

Just one of many photo ops at the start of the 1984 Olympics in Los Angeles.

The Smith family arrives at the '84 Games.

Here I am sporting my '83 World Championship gold and the Olympic gold medal from the relay in '84.

8

The 1984 Summer Olympics

Running in the 1984 Olympics in Los Angeles was something I had dreamed about. The honest-to-God Olympics, right here in the U.S.A! It was a very big deal for both the athletes and the fans after our boycott of the 1980 Games in Moscow. Finally, there would be a huge crowd for track and field at home. And my family would be there.

I had just graduated and gotten married and I was coming off a great year of running. In July of 1983, I had set a new world record at the National Sports Festival in Colorado Springs, for the 100 meter sprint, with a time of 9.93 seconds. I was officially the fastest man in the world.

Then, in early August of '83, at the inaugural World Championships in Helsinki, I placed first in the 200 meters with a time of 20.14. I was second in the

100 meters with a time of 10.21 seconds. Carl Lewis came in first at 10.07. Ben Johnson was bringing up the rear in sixth place at 10.44 seconds. I remember thinking that Carl probably had the better drugs on that day, although Ben claimed to be nursing a sore hamstring.

I was on the 4 x 100 meter relay team in Helsinki, along with Willie Gault, Emmit King and Carl Lewis. In that race, we set a new world record with a time of 37.86 seconds.

Also in August of '83, in the same evening at Weltklasse in Zurich, I became the first athlete to run under 10 seconds (9.97) for the 100 meters and under 20 seconds (19.99) for the 200 meters

I was thrilled with those times and felt invincible. Even though the Olympics in 1984 would cap off the year with gold, the season didn't start out well. I hurt my hamstring at Nationals that year and it wasn't completely healed by the Olympic Trials. The U.S. had six of the top ten sprinters in the world and it was going to be hard for me to make the team.

Through each round at the trials, my leg got worse and worse. It was by pure determination and the will of God that I even ran at all. I'd like to think it also had something to do with the fact that the rest of my body was in great condition, despite the hamstring.

My fourth place finish at the trials qualified me to be on the relay team at the Olympics with Sam Graddy, Ron Brown and Carl Lewis. I would run the third leg, as usual. But before the Games, there was a pre-Olympics race that I was required to run in. This relay was specifically for us to get our hand-offs and steps down for the real thing. I had no choice but to participate and I thought I could go all out. I was wrong and I re-injured my leg badly. However, I couldn't let anyone know because I knew I could lose my spot on the Olympic team.

I was thoroughly feeling the pain going into the Games, but I didn't moan or limp in public. Sidney Poitier and Mr. Luby would have been proud of my performance.

Thankfully, with the Games in Los Angeles, I didn't have to stay in the Olympic Village. I stayed with family. I had my father's California relatives. My wife traveled with me and my mother and some of my brothers and sisters came all the way from Mississippi. I was covered. I made sure to show no pain to anyone outside my inner circle. My wife says hiding the pain made me a grouch and they all stayed away from me to enjoy the other aspects of the Olympics. She understood the position I was in. I had three other runners depending on me.

I don't recommend this method of getting ready for the Olympics. It was reckless and selfish. I did what I needed to do for me and I was sure my determination would overcome my injury when the time came. And yes, I was haunted by all those thoughts about being the weak link during the race. What if I were the reason we lost the gold medal? It took a lot to push those thoughts out of my mind, but I did. Nothing was going to stop me.

At the start of the race, I mentally blocked out my injury. The crowd at the Los Angeles Coliseum was expecting our team to win big. We couldn't disappoint them. I concentrated on executing the race, getting the stick from Ron Brown and handing it off to Carl. I had to forget about my hamstring. Sam Graddy ran the first leg. We were in second place behind Australia when I got the baton from Ron, I didn't feel the pain. Adrenaline took over and I grabbed the lead with my subtle tilt in the turn, as all my former coaches had expected. I flew around that track until I handed off the baton to Carl. Then I felt the pain, but I still couldn't show it. When it was over and we had the gold medal, setting a new world record of 37.83 seconds, I think the pain miraculously went away. Or at least it felt that way.

For me, the reality of running and winning in the Olympics was better than the dream. I was so glad we were on American soil for this occasion. I had never heard a home crowd like this for any other meet. This was like a European crowd, loud track and field fans who knew us and loved us. It was the first time I felt that love from a stadium filled with boisterous Americans. My dream had come true. I was on the podium, getting an Olympic gold medal hung around my neck. People in the stands were going crazy. Then I remembered my wife was there and my mother. It was the only meet mother ever attended. The ultimate moment of achievement got even better as we stood to honor America with our national anthem. The U.S. team was winning it all at these Games. That was the plan.

I enjoyed our victory by living in the moment. I stood there appreciating all that my family, friends and coaches had done to help get me to this point. Knowing that, hey, I worked hard and ran through the pain and it had all been worth it, for Olympic gold.

That's what I thought about then and for years afterwards. It kept me from considering the truth of how Carl Lewis and his performance-enhancing drugs might have factored into this win. It's not like I had any control over it, or even any proof, but I believe we did not win cleanly. That's not to say that the other teams ran clean either, but I'll always consider this to be the "tainted" race of my career, not the one in Seoul in 1988.

There were a lot of celebrations to attend after they extinguished the Olympic flame in Los Angeles. There was a parade for me back home and all the local schools let the children out to attend. That was nice and I was happy to see so many familiar faces. My old buddy Bruce and his sister Mandy were there. Lots of my friends from the old neighborhood came out too. My dear friend Mildred Smith (no relation) was there. Miss

Jones, Miss Grenada and Miss Robinson, from church, looked so proud to welcome me home. It was everything you might expect from small-town America. I loved it and mother was over-the-moon. They told us, on the day of the parade, that they would be renaming the street I grew up on. *Calvin Smith Road* was the plan. But remember, things don't move quickly in the rural South. Over thirty years later, as far as I know, the sign still says Mt. Olive Road. But mother calls it "Calvin's street" when she's out and about in Bolton. Anyway, I guess it's the thought that counts. I'll never forget that wonderful day.

What I have often thought about too, over the years, is that the average American sports fan only sees a grand vision of the Olympics every four years. The opening ceremonies are elaborate spectacles. The networks do up-close and personal features on dedicated athletes so you know more than the score. They cater to the fact that those two weeks of coverage are when sports like track and field have to make their mark with future athletes as well as add to their fan base. In order to boost their ranks the USOC counts on a sense of national pride that usually comes with winning.

My perspective has been different. I saw the media coverage of track and field as being manipulated in the early '80s to get out the message that our whole organization was striving to get the drugs out of sports. I didn't see much real reporting going on.

I can't speak for others, but I was certainly aware that the so-called "random drug testing" often involved just the clean runners. I know I've peed a river for them. I know other athletes weren't tested nearly as often as those of us whom they knew could produce a clean test. No reporters ever picked up on that.

The public relations machines were spewing out details of how the tests were getting better at detecting more drugs and that was the big news. The USOC hyped how clean the Los Angeles Olympics would be because of better testing. They just didn't hype, or even release, the results of all their tests.

I remember that over half the U.S. sprint team tested positive for drugs at the trials for the 1984 Summer Games. If the rules had been adhered to, the drug users would have gotten a minimum three-months suspension from competing. That would have caused them to miss the Olympics. Can you imagine what that would have done to America's reputation when the Games were being held here at home?

What would it have done to our corporate sponsors? ABC reportedly paid $225 million for the rights to the Games. What about the sponsors the network had lined up for the two-week broadcast schedule?

The USOC that I came to know, was not willing to rock that boat filled with money. And, as far as I know, they didn't. The 1984 Summer Olympics was the first Games to make a profit since 1932. I guess the USOC felt an obligation to field the best team, regardless of the drug tests.

I don't doubt that it has probably happened in other countries too. Athletes using drugs to prepare to compete in the Olympics are doing all they can to get ready. That apparently includes cheating by taking, and trying to mask, banned substances.

The Olympic Trials, held two months before the Games, are when the athletes have to be at their best to make the team. If they are using drugs, their systems must be loaded at that time.

I believe everybody inside the sport of U.S. track and field in 1984 knew that nothing would be done about those positive tests. It was a given that athletes who graced the covers of Sports Illustrated magazine would not be banned from competing. In fact, the more popular an athlete became, the more untouchable he seemed to be.

I came to understand it's all about greed. People pay to see the stars. Sponsors pay to use the stars. Appearance fees go up for the stars. Everyone gets the money and recognition they want and the machine rolls on, moving like a steamroller over the athletes doing it the right way.

As far as I know, the sponsors were not actually spearheading the cover-up in 1984 or at any other time. But if so many of the athletes knew what was going on, someone at the top of all those companies had to at least hear the rumors. Of course, I understand it was in their best interest to look the other way. They were the ones financing the whole operation. They were the ones sponsoring the track meets locally, nationally and internationally. Then and today, the salaries of all the track and field governing bodies are directly connected to how much money the sport takes in from those sponsors. Whether it was television contracts, track apparel or commercials for heartburn medicine, if money was spent to promote track and field, the events had to look worthy. It was all about looking good and growing the sport. And it worked.

The more publicity and television time we had, the more athletes we attracted to track and field. College programs were getting bigger and better. More young people set their sights on landing a spot with our national team. But sadly, when those kids saw what was going on and how the drug users were winning, they either left the sport or got enticed to join the crowd. We've lost more healthy young athletes because of drugs than I care to count.

My friend Russ Rogers has been a track coach for forty-seven years. When he headed up a national team, he knew who the drug runners were. They came right out and told him, "Hey coach, I can't pass the drug test." Then he'd come to me or one of the other clean runners to fill the spot. He had to field a team and the tests just got in the way. So often, the tests had to be overlooked. It was crazy. To this day, with all his years on the track, Russ says he could not name a hundred runners on our national teams who ran clean. You do the math. That means not even two clean runners a year for forty-seven years!

Russ tells a story about the World Championships in Rome. One of his runners came to him and said, "Coach, I don't think I can pass the drug test." Russ says he was used to hearing this and told him to come along with him to see the team doctor. The guy was afraid to go. But Russ took him anyway and the runner told the doctor what he was on. The doctor was used to this too, and confirmed that he certainly wouldn't pass the test. So Russ had to take him off the team.

Another runner asked to replace him and Russ warned *this* guy of the upcoming drug test. Russ insisted that the new guy tell him the truth about whether he'd pass or not, because Russ had to officially declare the participants on his team. The new guy assured Russ he had nothing to worry about. Then, on the day of the test, he confessed he couldn't pass it. It seems the druggie was not yet a sponsored runner. He was in Rome with no money and if he got Russ to put him on the team, his hotel and meal expenses would be covered. That's typical druggie behavior. Russ couldn't do a thing about it.

I played it cool out in public. Nobody knew my groin was killing me.

Carl Lewis, me, Sam Graddy, Harvey Glance, Emmitt
King and Coach Mel Rosen.

The 1984 Olympic gold medal relay team. Ron Brown and Sam Graddy in back. Carl Lewis and me in front.

9

The RACE and the Sabotage

In August of 1988, one month before the Seoul Olympics, I came in second in the 100 meters at Weltklasse in Zurich. I ran 9.97. Carl Lewis won with a time of 9.93. Ben Johnson was third with a time of ten seconds flat.

Just four days later, at the IAAF Grand Prix Meet in Cologne, I was first in the 100 meters with a time of 10.16. The weather conditions were horrible and nobody was even thinking about record times. Dennis Mitchell, of the U.S., was second at 10.27, and Ben Johnson stopped trying when he saw he was only going to get third again. His time was 10.29. Carl Lewis skipped the whole event.

So, I was feeling good going into the Olympics. Beating guys who I knew were dopers was a real confidence-builder, especially right before the Olympics.

That's when I assume they were really loaded up with their "performance enhancers." Also, at the last Olympics, I was hurt and I didn't compete in the individual events. This time my training went smoothly and I was peaking at the exact time I had planned. I qualified for the 100 meters and would run the third leg of the 4 x 100 meter relay.

Veteran NBC sportscaster Charlie Jones and former Olympic marathon runner Frank Shorter were the commentators on the 100 meter event. Dave Sims was the trackside reporter.

When Ben Johnson crossed the tape with a new world record of 9.79, the stadium went wild. Ben kept running, over to a section of the crowd. Other runners, even Carl Lewis, followed to congratulate him. It looked like Carl had to actually grab Ben's hand in order to shake it. Ben was not offering it up to him.

I didn't feel the need to congratulate Ben, Carl or Linford Christie. They crossed the finish line before me because I believe they cheated with their "supplements" and that's not something I wanted to acknowledge with a sign of good sportsmanship. I headed for the exit. Ben and another Canadian runner took their country's flag for a victory lap around the track. Dave Sims grabbed media darling Carl for an interview on his second place finish. Here is part of that conversation from the broadcast:

Dave Sims: Did you see Ben at all? Did you feel his explosive start?

Carl Lewis: No, I didn't see him at all until about sixty or seventy meters down the tape. He must have caught a flyer because he was way out again, just like in Rome. But like I said, I think I could have done better. I just tried to run the best race I could and I'm pleased with my race.

After a commercial break, they came back to chaos at the side of the track with Dave Sims trying to get to me as Dennis Mitchell and I were being herded off the track by many of the South Koreans working the event.

Dave Sims: Calvin, Calvin, you finished fourth. Did you see Ben at all?

Calvin Smith: I was basically concentrating on my race and just trying to do my best.

Dave Sims: You came out shaking your head. What did you think?

I couldn't even answer because we were physically being pushed away from Dave. On the broadcast, people at home heard Charlie Jones and Frank Shorter laughing as they watched Dennis and I get farther away from Dave and his camera crew.

What I wanted to say to Dave Sims was this: I was in awe of both Ben's time and the circumstances of the event. I assumed that he and Carl were really drugged up for this race. What could you do? They were going to get away with it. How could this keep going on? I was also surprised at how well those drugs can work in the body and how Ben bounced back from losing to me twice, not so long ago. What an incredible time! That much time, a fraction of a second, makes a big difference. That little edge determines if you're first or eighth.

Those were the thoughts in my head, but I just couldn't allow them to come out of my mouth. Yes, that's what I wanted to say before I got pushed through the exit by the Koreans.

On the broadcast, Charlie and Frank continued with their analysis, using slow-motion and several angles of the race.

Frank Shorter: Ben Johnson gets another incredible start. That probably is the best 100 meters run, technically, start to finish. Before, we were always worried about how he finished. We were never worried about his start. Well, standard perfect start for Ben Johnson. Up, away, he is just away from everybody. The race is over right here, from fifty meters in. He is at full speed so much quicker than anyone else in the race. We knew he'd be ahead here (halfway point), but not so far. He's got three meters on Carl Lewis and I think Carl could see him at this point.

I had to agree. Carl *was* watching Ben.

Getting out of the blocks quickly, and your first thirty meters, can throw other athletes off their game, if they watched. And that's exactly why they don't watch. My start was never the best and that was okay. The latter part of the 100 meters was always my race, so I didn't care if someone started well. I didn't pay attention to the other runners. This was my ten seconds and I certainly wasn't going to ruin it by turning my head to look at anybody else. You can mess up your whole race by watching another runner. If you don't believe me, just ask second-place Carl.

Carl wouldn't admit it to Dave Sims, but the slow-motion replay from the front clearly shows Carl actually turning his head and looking at Ben three times in that ten-second span. Runners in their right mind don't normally do that. In my opinion, that shows just how drugged-up Carl was. He wasn't running his race. He was more concerned with Ben's race.

After Charlie and Frank's analysis, the broadcast goes back to the NBC studio. Host Bryant Gumbel admits NBC hyped the race, and rightly so, because it exceeded expectations. He continued the hype of Ben versus Carl, not even mentioning Great Britain's Linford Christie, who came in third, or me, the quiet American runner with the clean urine test who came in fourth. But before the next commercial break, there I am. The freeze frame on the last shot of the replay from the front angle of the race is of only two men, Ben and me, in the lane on his left. Whoa! I photobombed Ben Johnson in 1988. Fade to black. Cut to commercial.

Three days later, after Ben's disqualification, NBC obviously had to devote some air time to talking about drugs. They had Dr. Paul Thompson on the set with Bryant Gumbel. They called him their "sports medicine analyst." I wondered if they actually needed a "sports medicine analyst" before this scandal. At this point, the name of Ben's specific drug had not been released.

Bryant: Why would an athlete who had such a good chance at a gold medal take such a chance?

Dr. Thompson: Well, he had to make a mistake. What the athletes do is they use these substances to increase their muscle size, their muscle strength and their muscle power. And they stop them a period of time before competition. He either cut it too close, or somehow otherwise made a mistake that resulted in a positive test.

Listening to the doctor's matter-of-fact blanket statement, and inference to how all athletes use drugs, angered me. Some of us didn't use drugs to train or to compete. Didn't he know that? Why didn't he say anything about the clean runners? And then he went from Ben's possible mistake to a possible benefit of his "substances."

Dr. Thompson: They produce 'roid rage. They make you much more aggressive, more intense, and more interested in training hard.

Well, that I saw. They were intense. Ben Johnson and Carl Lewis hated each other. Everybody inside the sport knew it. Carl played it up as much as he could, for the publicity. Behind the scenes, it was no different. They really hated each other. Intensely. Carl's ego got deflated every time he crossed the finish line after Ben, which fed his hatred. And Ben just couldn't stand how Carl tried to position himself as the better athlete when Ben was beating him regularly. Those of us in-the-know thought it was clear that Ben had access to the better drugs. But both seemed to have enough in them to show evidence of rage.

Since that time in 1988, when the good doctor on NBC was spewing information on the benefits of 'roid rage, I have noticed it's no longer regarded as such a positive side effect of anabolic steroids. It has been used in criminal cases as a possible defense for accused murderers. It has also been linked to other illegal aggressive behavior and suicides. I wish smart young athletes would consider that before doping.

It's not a secret outside of track and field. You just have to use Google to come up with the real life sad stories in which 'roid rage has played a part. And doesn't it make sense? If what you put in your body has such a tremendous effect, won't it also have tremendous side effects? The research continues. (Note to scientists: It would be most efficient to look for research subjects inside the world of track and field.)

It seems to me that while the whole world was focused on record-breaking races, we were also watching our sport go downhill fast. These two runners, supposedly the fastest sprinters in the world, were cheating, according to the standards of those of us who took nothing to enhance our performances. The clean runners were watching from the sidelines. Oh, we were talking about them, but only to each other. That's all we could do and I think it helped. It was a release, like group therapy. We said things like, "If we were doping, we'd be unbeatable. The world records we'd set would be untouchable." But we weren't willing to cheat. We had principles and we had friends. That's what saved us.

We were talking about it for years before Ben and Carl ever got caught. After they got caught, when the reporters and the public started talking about it, it was old news to us. By then, we were tired of talking about it and even more tired of waiting for things to change. They never would.

It was unfortunate that the sprinting scandal overshadowed some of the other more positive stories at the Seoul Olympics. North Carolina State's Kay Yow, diagnosed with breast cancer the previous year, would coach the U.S. women's basketball team to a gold medal. The U.S. men's basketball team won the bronze with college kids. This was the last Olympics before the NBA offered up their best. And Greg Louganis continued his domination in diving with gold in the 3 meter and 10 meter events, despite suffering a concussion in the preliminaries. We didn't know it then, but his bloody accident on the board came a few months after he found out he was HIV positive. There were plenty of other stories at the Games too. But it was the drug found in the urine of the Canadian track star that stole the headlines.

On the same day as the men's 100 meters at the 1988 Games, Florence Griffith-Joyner set a new world record in the semifinals of the women's 200-meter sprint, then beat it for an even better time in the finals. September 23, 1988 could have been the greatest day ever in Olympic sprinting. Those of us on the inside knew it was a ridiculous sham. More about Flo-Jo later.

If you listened, watched and read everything that

came out after Ben's steroid moment, you might have seen the sabotage excuse. To the general public and even the American reporters who only cover track and field every four years, it was kind of dismissed as outrageous.

Ben had said that a friend of Carl Lewis was in the testing room with him after the race, before Ben peed in a cup. Ben says, after receiving congratulations from the FOC (Friend of Carl) for winning, he asked the guy to hand him his beer, which was already open and in the testing room. The FOC could have added the steroid to Ben's beer right then and there. And that, ladies and gentlemen, is one possible reason why Ben Johnson got caught with steroids in his system after the race. Of course another reason could be that he had been taking them for years.

I thought the sabotage excuse was outrageous too. They don't let just anyone in the testing room. And, if samples have to be kept pure, how did someone bring in any liquid, never mind a beer, into the room. Crazy, right? Crazy enough to be true.

After I participated in Daniel Gordon's 30 for 30 documentary film, 9.79, on ESPN in 2012, I got the rest of the story. It seems that the FOC, Andre Jackson, a member of Carl's Santa Monica Track Club, somehow got into the testing room. So did Ben's beer. Ben told the story on film and it went just like the hearsay the rest of us athletes laughed about so long ago. Ben said it happened and Jackson doesn't deny it.

So was this the Nancy Kerrigan-Tonya Harding moment of the 1988 Games? Did Carl send his buddy into the testing room to take out his competition and assure him of a medal? Remember, the race was over. Carl came in second. Carl knew that if Ben was disqualified, he'd get the gold medal. The one he so coveted to replace the 1984 gold medal he won for the 100 meters that he buried with his father in May of 1987. Maybe that's the real story.

I think anyone who knows Carl would say he's fully capable of orchestrating that. But I also believe we'll never know what really happened in that testing facility. What I know for sure is, no one believes a liar, even when he's telling the truth.

Even with my low-key demeanor, I managed to get a few magazine covers. This one is from October of 1983.

(courtesy Track & Field News)

And in December of 1987, Track & Field News put me on the cover again, as the World 200 Champion.

(courtesy Track & Field News)

10

Teamwork is Key

The casual track fan may not know this but, there are actually six runners designated for the four-man relay team. Sometimes the other two will run in the preliminaries. And if the team wins, they get awarded the same medals as those who run in the finals. The coaches for the Seoul Games often said to us that Carl Lewis would not be on the team if he didn't practice with the team. But back in 1984 he didn't, and he was. So much for the threats.

I guess it was hard for him to be a team player when he didn't seem to know the meaning of the word team. I never saw Carl care about anyone but himself, before, during and after his years on drugs. It didn't matter to me how he handled his individual events, but his ego was a big problem when it came to the 4 x 100 meter relay. Carl's attitude was, "I'm a superstar. I don't need to practice with *them.*" *Them* being three other world-class athletes who regularly practiced with each other without a problem. Unfortunately, most of the coaches gave in to him. I'm sure I wasn't the only one who felt it was unfair to the rest of us.

ABC did the '84 Olympics, broadcast from Los Angeles. It was those Games that the Soviet Union, East Germany and other nations boycotted, in retaliation for the U.S. skipping the 1980 Olympics in Moscow. That cut down on the competition. However, it might as well have been called the Carl Lewis Olympics. That's who ABC hyped before and during their coverage.

It might have helped that Carl's manager, Joe Douglas, opened his big mouth and compared Carl to music superstar Michael Jackson right before the Games. Here in the real world, no one but Joe and Carl thought that Carl was worthy of rock star status. The reporters had a field day with that remark and a sort of anti-Carl movement began. But all publicity is good publicity in Carl's camp.

Al Michaels and O.J. Simpson were the track and field commentators at the Los Angeles Coliseum. Say what you will about O.J., but I know he told the God's honest truth in 1984 when he reported that Carl's teammates were complaining about him not showing up for practice. Hey, even Michael Jackson rehearsed with his brothers. Of course when our team won the gold, the talk about Carl's sloppy practice regimen stopped, but only briefly. We knew it would happen again. Fast forward four years.

At the '88 Olympics in Seoul, Carl didn't run in the preliminaries because he had other events. That was understandable. That's why we had the other two guys. However, he had no excuse not to show up for practice for the relay. And because he didn't practice with us, the rest of us had to rotate around. It was difficult because there was no consistency. Naturally, there continued to be hard feelings because we all anticipated that Carl might get a spot in the finals. I'm not making excuses, but the non-team atmosphere did nothing to keep our eye on the prize. Preparing a relay team for an Olympic event is not supposed to be done this way.

Six names were submitted to run. Dennis Mitchell, Albert Robinson, Lee McNeill, and I ran in the preliminaries. Joe DeLoach and Carl Lewis were the other two names on the list. Coach Russ Rogers, not a fan of Carl, said that no practice meant no race. I have to admit that it would have been nice to see Carl sit during the finals, but we'll never know. We were disqualified during the preliminaries when Lee McNeill, running Carl's anchor leg, took off before I got to the exchange mark with the baton.

As bad as we all felt about it, we understood why it happened. It was just inexperience with Lee. He was young and he got excited. It was his first Olympics and he never should have been put in that position. I think that if Carl had practiced with us, Lee would have relaxed, knowing for sure Carl would take over in the finals. I firmly believe that. Then the U.S. would have had back-to-back gold medals in the 4 x 100 meter relay. Instead, we watched from the sidelines as the Soviet Union won, followed by Great Britain and France. They didn't touch our previous world record time.

As if the Soviet win wasn't enough, NBC added insult to injury by inviting Carl to the studio (with Bryant Gumbel, of course) to talk about the disqualification. You can just imagine how the rest of the team loved that.

NBC was probably just looking for a face to put on television, and Carl was always willing to be that face. Since I'm sure Carl was mad at Coach Rogers for threatening to leave him off the team for not practicing, this NBC move provided the perfect opportunity for him to rub it in to Russ. Looking at file video, Carl and Bryant compared our '84 gold medal race to this preliminary run and Carl noted how the handoffs were not as smooth this time. Keeping in true Carl form, he didn't take any responsibility for that. Commenting on my leg of the race, giving me credit, Carl said, "Calvin absolutely explodes!" Little did he know that's exactly what I would have done, had I been invited to the studio with him.

I saw that many athletes in the world of track and field didn't care for Carl Lewis. Outwardly, there was nothing likeable about him, even before the "performance enhancers" turned him into a drugged-up winner on the track. He presented himself as if he had the greatest ego of all time and, the attention he got for speaking out about himself, just fed that ego. He acted like a superstar who wanted to be insulated by his posse even before he had a posse.

As far as I can tell, all that attitude has backfired on him in real life. After the '84 Olympics, He didn't get all those endorsement deals he and his manager, Joe Douglas, thought he would. Pepsi commercials starred the real Michael Jackson.

The only thing Carl Lewis got after winning nine Olympic gold medals, was a boatload of more awards that didn't seem to generate any income. He's been named Olympian of the Century by Sports Illustrated, Athlete of the Century by the IOC, World Athlete of the Century by the IAAF and a bunch more, voted on by folks who obviously didn't know, or care, how he got his medals. I've always wondered how that happened, since he admitted to doping during his running years before getting some of those awards.

Looking back at all he did, and seeing all he doesn't have now, only makes me more content with my own life. Although I'll never understand why he acted the way he did and why he doped up and tarnished our sport. That was just wrong on so many levels. But as my wife says, "You can't fret over what other people do. It catches up with them."

The Smith family portrait in 1988.

We took Brittney and Calvin II to see the Olympic
Games in Atlanta in 1996.

Calvin II (on the left) was on Team USA at the Games in Beijing. The other young man is the 2008 Olympic decathlon champion Bryan Clay.

11

Talk is Cheap

It never crossed my mind to put my career and my health in jeopardy to win a race or a medal. And I certainly wouldn't do anything that would embarrass my dear mother or all my coaches and teammates who knew what I could do with my God-given ability and hard work. The idea of winning always influenced the amount of effort I made and the way I trained, but was never important enough for me to load up on drugs. It was the journey, the lifestyle, and the thrill of running that really mattered to me. Winning was a bonus that I thoroughly enjoyed with a clean body and a clean conscience.

That made it very hard for me to accept what was going on within my sport. It was difficult too, for me to tolerate what the media was reporting with regard to drugs. Back in the 80s, they often pointed out that the accuracy of the drug tests for all athletes was questionable. It didn't get much more negative than that. Most reports reflected the view of the official track and field organizations who were feeding the media and could only be hurt by real evidence. They were not about to give up their best runners. So, I think Ben Johnson was lulled into a false sense of security throughout his career. He probably thought everyone would cover for him as long as he kept his sponsors and his Canadian coaches happy.

On the other hand, maybe he didn't think about it at all. I wondered if he could even think straight. Since the drugs were obviously affecting his body, I had to question what they were doing to his mind. He was supported and handled by his doctors, agents, coaches, sponsors, worldwide track and field officials, and even the Olympic Federation, except for that one race in 1988. Did he even have the ability to think for himself?

Although I didn't like what he was doing, I liked Ben. He was a regular guy, very down-to-earth. In the early days, before anyone suspected he had started taking steroids, I beat him all the time. He was not one of the runners you worried about. Neither was pre-steroid Carl. But after Ben started beefing up and running on drugs, he'd have to have a really bad day and I'd have to have my best day ever, to stay on his heels.

It was evident to me that I wasn't running against a man. I was running against a finely-tuned, chemically-fueled machine. Up close, you could clearly see the change in him. He seemed to be in another world. The whites of his eyes were yellow and his pupils were kind of darting here and there. But he still talked to everyone and he always signed autographs for the fans.

Ben was humble. He didn't crave superstardom the way Carl Lewis did. Even when he left the 1988 Olympics in shame, he was traveling with his mother.

She raised a very nice son, except for the cheating, of course.

Even though we were never close, I could tell Ben was very conflicted about what he was doing when he was doing it. There were many times he denied using drugs, despite the positive urine tests. To me, a denial about testing positive, shows guilt. Like so many other athletes, he had a bag full of excuses to pull from as to how those tests might have turned out positive. Only the guilty need excuses.

I almost feel sorry for Ben, but not because of all the chaos that surrounded him. He was responsible for his own un-doing. I feel sorry for him because somehow he lacked the integrity to play it straight and I don't understand why. How could a man who had a supportive family and friends, and the backing of his country, lack the character to hold his head high, play fair and do right by them? I doubt Ben Johnson has ever known the feeling that comes with winning the right way. That's why I almost feel sorry for him. Almost. I wonder how far he would have gotten on his raw talent and a good running program.

For years I watched Ben being promoted as the highlight of all the meets. He was considered the best athlete in the world and people thought he was doing something that no one else could do. The media touted him as the unbeatable guy who would win any race that he entered. Everybody should have known it was too good to be true. And when the truth came out, Ben kept changing the spin on his story. He was the Lance Armstrong of track and field.

You can look up any number of Ben Johnson videos on the internet and hear him talk about his drug use. Sometimes he says he's ashamed and should have been punished. Sometimes he says he needed to take drugs to be on a level playing field with the East Germans. He claims the drugs didn't make him run faster, only train harder. He says he was sabotaged in

1988 and wants to "clear his name." Not too long ago, he did an interview with the Wall Street Journal where he said he now advocates healthy eating and supplements. He didn't elaborate on the supplements. Ben says a lot of things.

Sometimes it bothered me that the drug runners always got to talk. Their lies were reported and broadcast. Me, I had the truth and no one cared.

When Ben broke my 9.93 record in the 100 meters at the World Championships in Rome in 1987, I did a very short interview with the BBC (British Broadcasting Corporation). They simply asked for my reaction. I said, "It was something I had been expecting, based on a few facts. I still consider myself the best runner." And that was the end of the interview. I guess they didn't care what my facts were or why I still thought I was the best. Or else, they knew I couldn't, and wouldn't, talk about it. And they probably couldn't get any proof if I did.

After our running careers were over, Ben and I were thrown together in 2004 when we appeared on a Japanese game show. We had a lot of time to fill at rehearsal because we were just a small part of the show. I told him about my family and how I had a job in the real world. He told me about his mom and his sister and how they were moving into a new house. It was normal, polite conversation between two guys waiting to face death in a swimming pool. More about that soon.

I was actually enjoying our conversation until he told me he was going out on a lot of speaking engagements. I asked him what he talked about. He said he talked about the benefits of not taking drugs. I remember I shot him a sarcastic grin. I swear he didn't even notice. I honestly think Ben believes what he says when he says it. He kept talking and I kept smiling. He was seriously telling me, the-always-clean-running Calvin Smith, that he was talking to young people about staying off drugs!

What could I say to the guy who was one of the biggest druggies out there and who has lied about cheating so many times? What does he know about playing fair and working hard to compete without drugs? Who writes those speeches for him? What the hell kind of organization would book him as an anti-drug speaker?

It took all of my self-control not to say it out loud. I felt the same way as I do now. I'm your anti-drug speaker. I've got the experience. I not only ran clean, I did it in the middle of a circus full of drugged-up Ben Johnsons. I get frustrated just thinking about it.

As I said earlier, the Japanese game show involved Ben and me facing death in a swimming pool. That's how it looked to me anyway.

I'll probably always have the competitive spirit. I want to win no matter what the contest. But even if you offered me a ton of money and a truck filled with my favorite foods, I still wouldn't bet on me in a swimming contest. I sink like lead. There is no buoyancy in this body and my technique could only be described as flailing.

Living in Tampa, Florida, with two kids, it was necessary to put a swimming pool in the backyard. At least that's what my wife and kids told me. I was out-voted. I hate water. I don't have anything to do with it. Don't swim. Don't want to. At the Summer Olympics in '84 and '88, I watched some of the swimming events in awe, knowing I could never do any of that. A nice shower is enough for me.

It has been suggested to me that my fear of swimming holes might be attributed to growing up without a father. Nobody threw me into a lake or a pool to teach me how to swim when I was little. That's how kids learned to swim in the old days. There were no lakes in Bolton and nobody had a pool. And I was born much too early for those crazy baby swim classes they have today. In fact, I managed to avoid all pools until a Japanese television producer phoned me in 2004.

In case you've forgotten, let me remind you again how much worldwide fame track and field athletes enjoy outside the United States. They love us in Japan, even more as we get slower and older. (If you're an American, think Joe DiMaggio and Johnny Unitas.) This was my seventh visit. I had traveled to Japan for various track meets throughout my career. And before the '88 Olympics, our track and field team trained there for two weeks before we flew on to Seoul for the Games.

Ben and I had been asked to appear, on television, in a race against other "celebrity" contestants. I was intrigued. The money was good and the trip was a first class vacation to Japan. How could I have refused? All I knew was, it was one of those crazy shows where the races aren't exactly what you expect. But hey, it was a free trip to Japan!

When we got to the studio on the first day, and I found out a swimming pool was involved, I wanted to pay them to let me go home. Yes, the race was going to be in a very long pool, six feet deep. That's two inches over my head. I was going to be totally under water, wearing scuba gear, weighted down, to run this race on foot. I imagined the next day's headline would read, "Gold Medalist Calvin Smith Drowns on TV Show in Japan."

We had to beat the clock in going against the other competitors. We weren't going to be in the pool at the same time. That was another drawback, because when I was in the pool, all eyes would be on me. I couldn't give in to a panic attack. I would just have to go through with it.

We had a few practice rounds "to get comfortable," they said. But every time I got in the pool I was praying hard and making deals with Jesus not to let me drown.

When the show went live, the track fans were

116

screaming for Ben and me. I'd like to think they saw me try to win, but I was actually just trying to control my breathing and stay calm enough to make it out alive. I didn't post the slowest time, but I was relieved I didn't make it to the finals. I didn't want to have to get in that pool ever again. Ben made the finals, even though he looked uncomfortable in the pool too. Some other celebrity I didn't even recognize was the winner.

My obvious clumsiness was a hit with the audience, so they invited me back the next year without Ben. This time it was a different game show and I knew enough to ask about the water situation before I accepted. This would be an indoor obstacle course and we had to clean it as we went through it. It was an awkward way to race and a younger man than I would do it faster, so I lost again. But at least I didn't have to call upon the Lord to save me, and I got another paid vacation to Japan, the Land of the Rising Sun and Crazy Television Shows.

As for Ben these days, as far as I know he spends his time doing a little coaching. And he's still going out on speaking engagements to talk about staying off drugs. He's tried some business ventures, but sadly for him, none of them have worked out. He's got a granddaughter now. I wish him the best.

I never feared running on dry land like I
feared that swimming pool.

I know my training schedule can help other runners. At the end of this book, there is information on how you can follow these workouts yourself.

12

Motivation

Even with all the drug turmoil in track and field in the 1980s, I enjoyed running so much. It was a way to relax my mind and think about things that I wanted to do. It was never a pressure thing. I would show up for a meet knowing that I had worked hard during the fall season, which is the off-season, to get into the best shape that I could. I'd go into the winter and spring ready to run. I was a lover of the sport who delighted in the fact that I could make money doing something that I truly enjoyed.

Like any other athlete, I didn't like losing, but early in the season, I didn't mind losing so much because my goal was to be at my best by the end of the season for the big events. In fact, I always saw the beginning of the season as the time to work on things and improve. Whatever happened at the early meets was okay with me, since I had time to get my race together for later on. Also, getting beat early in the season was a good motivator. I think it helped me to be successful when it counted the most.

Overall, my running career was a great experience. I had tremendous support from my wife, my mother and my in-laws. Our kids were always with us or them, and Melanie and I traveled the world. I wouldn't change a thing. I worked hard, peaked at the right time and was honored to represent my country at two Olympics. I even enjoyed running when I was one of the oldest guys on the track. Along the way, there has always been something that inspired me to do my best.

Understandably, right near the top of the list of what motivates me and most athletes is the fans. I know I've mentioned it before, but track and field in Europe is like football, baseball and basketball combined here in the U.S.A. It's like soccer there. It's truly amazing how the Europeans create such an intense atmosphere at track meets. It really gets you psyched up. You want to run for them.

They seem to know most track athletes like Americans know the New York Yankees. They are aware of our records, our times in the big meets, how we come off the blocks. They watch us and report on us and feature us in the headlines all year long. Even now, years into retirement, after Ben Johnson and Carl Lewis have been outed as drug users and I've quietly gone on to a normal life, if the three of us showed up at a track meet in Europe today, I believe we'd be hailed as a returning heroes.

It doesn't seem that long ago, at a meet in Italy in the early '90s, I learned that the winner would get his award from Pope John Paul II. This became a real motivating factor for me. Quite honestly, I didn't and still don't look at any man as better, or more holy, than anyone else, even the Pope. But I do admire him for what he does and what he represents. His is a position worthy of respect and I wanted to meet him. Not only that, I also thought about how my mother would love to tell the story of her son Calvin and the Pope. That was as good a reason as any for me to want to win.

My main competition in that race was Dennis Mitchell. He's five years younger than I am and yet another athlete who has admitted to making bad choices when it came to doping. In other words, he cheated. He was also a bit of a showboat on the track. He liked an audience and I'm sure he thought he was going to get his picture taken with the Pope. I'm also sure he wasn't worried about me, since I was on the downside of my career.

So there we were, about ten seconds away from having a Kodak moment that our grandchildren would cherish. From the second we left the blocks, I knew I had him beat. My family loves that picture of me and the Pope almost as much as I loved beating a drugged-up runner to get it.

As for meeting the Pope, well, it was interesting. He took my hand and placed the trophy in it. We smiled for pictures and he spoke to me. At least I think he spoke to me. He moved his lips. I saw that. He moved his lips for several moments. I smiled and nodded.

Later, when people asked me what he said, I wanted to be able to tell them something profound, but I couldn't. He spoke so softly that I didn't hear a word he said. Not a sound. And I couldn't make something up. If I lied about what I didn't hear the Pope say, I know I'd go straight to hell. But I was still honored to have gotten the award from him. Mother had her story and I have my picture. I'll admit, I feel blessed.

A lot of the races I won in my twilight years came down to motivation. Just give me a reason.

There was a runner named Jon Drummond who I am confident helped me win a race in Italy near the end of my career. In my later years on the track, I was never really sure of my ability. Sometimes the Olympic medalist and world record holder showed up and sometimes it was just plain old Calvin Smith, a race or two away from retirement.

Drummond is seven years younger than I am and although he's from Philadelphia, he went to school at Texas Christian University and quickly adopted the Texas way. You know, bigger and better. He was another showboat. Come to think of it, maybe it was the Philadelphia in him that made him a showboat too.

It was like the scene in that movie *Rocky*, when Rocky is running up those museum stairs. There was Drummond, playing to the crowds as he warmed up. I swear you could hear *Gonna Fly Now* when he turned it on. He milked the applause as he was introduced in the blocks, pumping his fists even before the announcer finished saying his name. He was just one of the best showboats I ever saw.

I'd like to say I noticed him showboating out of the corner of my eye, but no, I was watching him intently just like everyone else in the stadium. I was thinking he may have looked like a winner to the crowd, but to me, he looked like someone who needed to be taken down a notch. I thought it was time for him to learn a lesson in humility.

It was almost our start time for the 100 meters. We lined up in the blocks. Drummond was known to be a fast starter. I wasn't, except for this one day. I don't think I ever enjoyed a race so much. I glided through the tape and I swear he was huffing and puffing and dragging in second place. His fists were unclenched and he was a lot calmer than the showboat who started the race. He probably didn't see it that way, but I did — he was my motivator and I was his terminator.

Now that I think about it, Italy alone was a big reason I loved to run. I'd keep running forever if it meant more trips to Italy. Whenever we were there, the weather was nice and warm. Not hot, just warm. The food was really great. Their pasta was so fresh. It's different than the pasta I get everywhere else. And after a race, they fed us well. Maybe I'm exaggerating, but it always seemed like we had nine-course meals in Italy.

The bread is so much better in Italy too. I don't get up for breakfast here at home, but over in Italy, I'd get up early just to have bread with butter or jelly. I remember seeing trucks out on the streets with bread loaves piled high, not even covered. I often thought, that can't be the wonderful bread I'm eating here. But it was. It's basically traveling from the bakery to the cafes in the back of a pickup truck. I probably wouldn't eat bread from off the back of a truck here at home. But in Italy, I'd chase a truck for it. Once you've tried it, you've got to have it. Just don't think about where it's been.

My wife loved the Italian food too. In fact, on one trip she decided she was going to become a great Italian cook when we got home. At a tourist shop, she excitedly picked up a bunch of beautiful cookbooks with big pictures of mouth-watering dishes. It wasn't until we unpacked at home that she realized the recipes were written in Italian. They make nice coffee table books.

I stopped competing in 1996 and in those last few years, I guess it was mostly the food that kept me going. I had seen the sights many times and won enough medals, but there were more restaurants to conquer.

In France, I couldn't get enough of the pastry shops and Melanie loved the brioche. We especially liked Nice and all the small towns along the French Riviera where you could eat at an outdoor café and watch the yachts anchored there or bobbing around in the Mediterranean Sea.

One year I took my family to the French Riviera at Christmas. I told them I wanted them to come with me in the off-season because I couldn't devote a lot of tourist time to them when I was racing. But honestly, I crossed the ocean for those French pastries. The strawberry tarts are my favorite. I never had such wonderful, sweet strawberry tarts like that, not even from my mother's kitchen. And that's high praise.

SPORTS
In brief

From staff and wire reports

Pope watches Smith win 100

Pope John Paul II made pontifical history Sunday by watching the 100-meter dash at an international track meet in Formia, Italy, and awarding first prize to U.S. sprinter Calvin Smith of Bolton.

The race was held in John Paul's honor during his 81st pastoral trip inside Italy, taking him to Formia, about 80 miles south of Rome on the Mediterranean seacoast, and to nearby Gaeta and Itri.

In his white papal robes and skullcap, John Paul bestowed first prize on Smith, a former 100-meter world champion, who won the race with a time of 10.25 seconds.

Calvin Smith receives his award from Pope John Paul II.

Me and Pope John Paul II, perhaps the two quietest guys in Formia, Italy on that particular day. My winning time was 10.25 seconds. Mother was happy to add this page to her Calvin scrapbook.

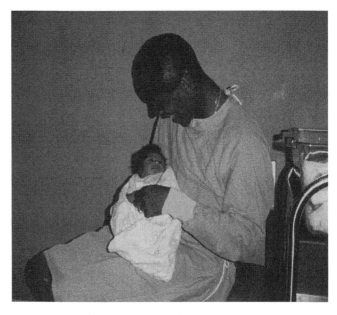

And here's another blessing, our first baby, Brittney.

Brittney, all grown up and a Florida A & M college graduate.

CALVIN SMITH
Alabama

One of the finest 100 and 200 meter competitors in history, Calvin Smith captured five individual Drake Relays titles. He won the university/college 100 in 1982, while anchoring Alabama to victories in the 4x100 and 4x400 relays. He was named the outstanding performer of the 1983 Drake Relays after setting a university/college record in the 100 while running on Alabama's 4x100 and sprint medley relays, which set meet records. Smith ran the 200 leg on the sprint medley relay that set a National Collegiate and American record of 3:17.19. He captured the invitational 200 at the 1984 Drake Relays and swept the invitational 100 and 200 in 1985. In 1988 he was inducted into the Drake Relays Hall of Fame. He set a world record in the 100 (9.93) in 1983 and was a two-time world champ in the 200 (1983, 1987). Smith won a gold medal in the 1984 Olympics running on the 4x100 relay and captured a bronze medal in the 100 at the 1988 Olympics.

100
Drake Relays Athlete of the Century

Recognition made possible by
Meredith Corporation Foundation

Calvin II has been following in my footsteps since he graduated from the University of Florida. Here he is at my Drake Relay Hall of Fame plaque. I was inducted in 1988.

13

Off the Track

My last year of competing was 1996. My final race was in a meet at LSU (Louisiana State University). I was thirty-six years old and simply strained a leg muscle while running. At the moment it happened, I said to myself, "That's it. It's over." It was an easy decision. I was experienced enough to know recovering from that injury to run again would have pushed my body beyond its natural limits. I didn't even consider resorting to a drugged-up recovery program like some other runners might have done. My racing days were over. I'd had a good run (pun intended) and I felt it was time for me to give back.

I wanted to stay involved in sports, so I became an assistant coach at Alabama where I stayed for two years. I enjoyed coaching, even though the talent wasn't of high caliber at Alabama at that time. The young athletes, however, were good people and they were committed to doing their best for the Crimson Tide. It was refreshing to finally be away from all the druggies in professional track and field. Yes, I see the irony in that I had to go back to college to get away from drug users.

My family and I went back to Tampa, Florida in 1998, since it had been our home base after Melanie and I graduated. Anheuser-Busch was one of the U.S. companies that hired potential Olympic athletes in jobs that also allowed for training time. I had worked for them as a purchasing agent, based in Tampa, while I was doing all that European travel.

Now that my running career was over, looking for a real job in Tampa was not that easy. Perhaps it was more difficult for me because, even with a college education, I didn't know what I wanted to do. I had been careful with my money, except for that one time in my youth when I bought a BMW. (I drive a Toyota now.) I had a house and most everything my family needed, but it didn't make sense for me to just wait for my dream job to come along because I had no idea what that would be. So I looked for a job that would give me a regular salary, benefits and some experience in dealing with people. After all, I had a degree in public relations.

With the best of intentions, I started working for the state of Florida in the department of children and families. That was a learning experience. I worked with people who needed cash assistance and food stamps. I liked the idea of helping others who were having a hard time, but eventually I got tired of the complaints I had to deal with on the job, and I decided it was time to move on.

My next job was with Goodwill. I was a case manager and it was my responsibility to see that people worked for their cash assistance. They could have a paying job or a volunteer job, but they had to work. Once again, I was learning what I didn't want to do for a living. But I still liked the idea of helping people.

Next, I decided to become a teacher. I got a temporary certificate and the job that not many teachers in their right mind would take. I was going to teach Language Arts to a class of juvenile delinquents in an alternative-to-an-alternative school. In other words, these are the kids who were thrown out of public school, went to the bad boy school, and got thrown out of that too. So now they were at the school that was one step above lock-up.

It's no wonder the opening came smack in the middle of the school year. Someone had left this job quickly. But that didn't faze me. I figured I was going to get to play my man Sidney Poitier again — this time in *To Sir, With Love*. However, on my first day, that dream quickly died. They were a rough and rowdy bunch and my only thoughts were, "What have I gotten myself into and will I make it home tonight?"

But you know what? They liked sports. So I used my background to reach out to them. I also learned a lot from them about the judicial system, because they liked to share their stories too. At the end of the school year, unharmed and confident I was contributing, I signed up for another tour of duty. After I made it out alive again the next summer, I decided not to push my luck and moved on. I was genuinely surprised that no one sang their thanks to me on the last day of school, like Lulu did for Sidney. Melanie said that was asking too much.

The next school year, I got a job in a regular public middle school. It was wonderful, and a little more relaxing compared to where I had just been. I had the low-level kids and I found it very rewarding to work with them. It was important to me to always try to inspire them and connect with them in some way they would remember.

There was one girl in my first class who had no confidence in doing school work. Someone had convinced her she couldn't do anything. I told her, "I'm going to work with you and you are going to pass my class." She worked hard and she passed. I was happy enough with that, but when she came back to thank me, well, that was really something.

I spent two more years at that middle school, recognizing that my career in track was a big factor in my success as a teacher. Plus, the confidence you get after you know you have reached just one kid, gives you the motivation to keep reaching out to the next kid. I didn't let the little things get me down. I appreciated there was always someone else to help, like there was always another race to run.

One day at school I overheard some teachers talking about a rich, spoiled brat that no one wanted in their class. I didn't know her, but wondered how bad could she be? I survived the alternative-to-alternative school. Well, I soon found out when she ended up in my class. She was a handful, but you know what? She wasn't *that* bad. Her enabling parents were the problem. They had every excuse in the book for her behavior and I wasn't buying it. According to them, I was too strict. So they eventually took her out of my class. After that, she would come back to my room just to talk to me. I think I was the only one who didn't let her get away with anything. She was looking for someone to be concerned about her and to hold her accountable. I got a lot out of that.

I never did finish getting my teaching certificate. I didn't pass the math test so I moved on to non-profit agencies next, working with ex-offenders and HIV and AIDS patients who needed assistance. I was even a housing supervisor once. I actually had to talk landlords into taking tenants who were ex-offenders and HIV positive. That was a challenge. As you might imagine, some of those criminals were drug users. I did my best to help those who were working towards a better life. But when they didn't live up to their end of the deal in qualifying for assistance, it was tough. It's not like I didn't understand their predicament, but they needed to follows the rules and guidelines of the program.

Another part of my job as a housing supervisor

was to do random checks to make sure the ex-offenders were not still offending. One time, when I walked into a client's apartment, and it was full of people high on drugs. I have to admit that seeing them led me to feel some pent-up hostility, as I was reminded of the drugged-up cheaters who beat me on the track. And even though I was half the size of some of those junkies, I told them all to get out and I got the client thrown out of the program as well. If only I could have done that on the track.

I currently work with a non-profit agency helping to provide people with medical assistance. I enjoy what I do. As you know by now, I like talking to people and giving encouragement. I like telling them, and helping them to believe that no matter what their situation is, they should always have hope. I'm not sure if this will be my last career move, but it's a job that I feel very good about doing.

Our two children are grown now. As a father, I kept them sheltered from the dirty business side of track, like my family in Bolton kept me sheltered from racial discrimination. I guess you could call it the need-to-know system of parenting.

They both ran track in college and we greatly appreciated those athletic scholarships. We were also relieved to know that they were spending their free time, after class, on the track and at the gym. Our daughter, Brittney, left the sport after she graduated from Florida A & M. But our son, Calvin II (Calvin Two), is still running after graduating from the University of Florida in 2014.

Calvin II had a tremendous amount of success as a Gator, and is doing very well as a pro. He earned a school record eighteen All-American titles at Florida. He's been on our Olympic Team, and is part of the 4 x 400 Indoor World Record Relay Team along with Kyle Clemons (University of Kansas), David Verburg (George Mason University), and Kind Butler III (Indiana

University).

I'd like to think Calvin II inherited his gift of speed from me. These days, he's keeping me busy as a "volunteer" track coach. I tell him to train hard and run his race. Don't worry about the cheaters. That's my advice to all the up-and-coming track stars. Just run your race. There is nothing you can do about the dopers, so don't waste your energy even thinking about them. As long as Calvin II does his best, that's all he can do for himself, and that's all his mother and I expect.

When I'm at the track with him, other runners recruit me for coaching too. I'm happy to help for now. It's a joy to watch athletes achieve their goals, especially when I see them getting better with my coaching. But I look forward to the day when my time is my own.

Coaching is very demanding and it takes a lot out of me. It's not just technique. You have to handle their emotions too. Calvin II dissects every part of his race. He must have gotten that trait from his mother's side of the family. I tell him, "Stop worrying and just run." Calming guys down and building them up is hard work. Not everybody has the laid-back attitude I enjoyed.

Calvin II graduated with a degree in sociology. I think his career in track and field will provide him with quite a thesis if he ever decides to do any post-graduate work. He's learning plenty about people, organizations and society while he's traveling and running for the U.S. National Team.

In addition to his speed, I think he also inherited my talent for listening. He tells me an awful lot about the runners from other countries. We've had several discussions about the perks for which he's not eligible. He sees runners from the small independent islands and tiny nations getting treated like royalty by their governments. They get land, houses, farm animals, whatever makes them happy, as long as they put their homeland on the map with the IAAF and the IOC. Once they retire, they are set up for the rest of their lives. That doesn't happen to a kid born and raised in Florida, even if he is a world-record holder. Calvin II has had to accept the fact that he will never be King. On the bright side, he's young and healthy, has a job he loves, and he's seeing the world without me paying for it. Melanie and I help him out when he's on the road by taking care of our grand-dog, an Akita named Kojo.

These young track stars are working hard and competing the right way. Calvin Smith II, Stanley Suber Jr., Austin Lewis, Mario Briscoe, and La'Shae White.

I hope Calvin II gets as much out of travelling the world as I did. Here I am feeding a baby kangaroo in Australia, bribing it to perform for my video camera.

I'm comfortable on the sideline these days. That's me with a couple of other Alabama athletes, Stacy Bowen and Lillie Leatherwood.

Awards for what I've done in my career are made extra special when I can share them with my children.
(courtesy John Elliott *Studio*)

My lovely co-workers who never knew the quiet
Calvin. Left to right, they are Marisol Leon, Kendra
Keaton and Crystal Thomas.

14

Performance Enhancement

Performance-enhancing drugs. I only use that term sarcastically, or when I'm quoting others, usually sports reporters. When clean athletes are talking about other athletes being on drugs, the word drugs implies that the athlete is taking something to make him run faster. That's cheating, and that athlete is nothing but a druggie to us. And druggie means user, doper, junkie, and addict. Some of us have no need for a euphemism.

If you've ever spent any time watching runners compete, you can see how they look at the beginning, middle, and end of a race. We hold tightly-wound energy as we step into the blocks. That's why the false start is forgiven, once. The middle of a race is all acceleration, faster and faster to the finish line.

Take a look back at some of the races won by Ben Johnson, Carl Lewis and others who have tested positive for drugs. There's a certain ease to their stride. Other runners can see it. It's unnatural. The human body, in its purest form, is not built to maintain speed. Endurance has its limits too. Both speed and endurance come a little easier with aptly named performance-enhancing drugs.

It doesn't take a genius, or even a doctor, to tell if someone is on drugs. Just ask any high school teacher or the parent of a rebellious teenager. You may not be able to cite the blood level numbers or even test the urine, but you know. You just know.

The noticeable gain of muscle mass is one telltale sign. A runner is not built like The Hulk when he starts out in the sport. If he were, some high school coach would redirect him to the weightlifting team or the football field long before he tried to qualify for an Olympic sprint event.

Back in September of 1988, during the NBC Olympic broadcast on Ben Johnson's steroids, sports commentator Dwight Stones (1972 Olympic bronze medalist in the high jump) told Bryant Gumbel, "This is not a substance abuse problem. This is a chemical enhancement of performance. But it is illegal in events. But it is not cocaine abuse or other things that our professional counterparts are suffering from."

The drug news in the headlines at the time centered on baseball players like Darryl Strawberry and Steve Howe and their cocaine problems.

We reached out to Dwight Stones via email while writing this book to talk about what he said then, and to ask about what he thinks of the continuing "chemical enhancement of performance" today. His response was, "A conversation with someone I do not know about something that took place more than a quarter century ago is not a priority for me." Dwight is still in the sports game, running sports camps and working as a personal high jump coach, according to his website. I've also seen him on television doing commentary for track and field.

As I've said before, the system is all about greed and growth and not biting the hand that feeds you. I know it because, when I made a living on the track, I was fully embedded too. Follow the money and it leads to an organization with too much leverage over people. It would take a huge reversal of priorities to change how the big machine of track and field operates.

Professional athletes are not blind or stupid. They see everything that's going on in their sport, whether they speak up about it or not. And they know more than the public will ever know. Changes in someone's physical appearance and their running times don't happen overnight, or even from one season to the next. Traveling and competing with the same men and women all year long gives every athlete plenty of opportunity to spot the changes.

Prior to the Games in 1988, the word was out among those of us in the track and field community that Florence Griffith-Joyner might be on drugs. Her body had obviously changed quickly and dramatically. No one could deny that. The company line was that she had changed her diet and started on a weightlifting program. I hadn't seen her in-person for a while and then ran into her at a meet in Oregon. I was waiting in front of the elevator at the hotel, talking to people. The doors opened and, before I turned around, I heard a very deep voice say, "Hey, Calvin!" I thought it was a man talking to me, but Florence was the only one looking at me. It was her voice and it was not a woman's voice anymore. I remember wondering if it was possible for diet and weightlifting to have any impact on vocal cords.

Although the public record shows she never had a positive drug test while competing, I think I've already made my point about the drug tests that Olympic athletes have taken and what can be done with them. I know that since Flo-Jo's death from an epileptic seizure in 1998, her husband, Al Joyner, has publically stated, even on Oprah, that her autopsy was the ultimate drug test. But she died ten years after she stopped competing. Everything I've read says steroids wouldn't show up in a body ten years later.

I know what I saw and I know what I heard. Yes, I guess I could be wrong. I'm not God and I don't know what people do behind closed doors. But I was there at that elevator and I was around Flo-Jo many times before that.

Even though my personal opinion never counted when I was inside the big track and field machine, now that so much has come to light about cheating athletes, I hope you will consider the source. At the very least, I hope people will always consider Calvin Smith to be a credible source.

Did you ever notice how many runners get braces on their teeth as adults? I used to wonder how they got past the growth spurt of puberty without braces, and then suddenly, a new growth spurt in their adult mouths was so troubling that it forced them to metal-up. I learned that human growth hormone (HGH), which is said to increase muscle mass, can account for that. It makes things, like the jaw, grow bigger. Carl Lewis had braces at the 1987 World Championships in Rome. And he's not the only one. I'll bet there were more runners with braces on the track with me at some national meets than there were on all the American teenagers in the high school auditoriums I've spoken in. Is it a coincidence that I competed against an awful lot of people with crooked teeth? I found it peculiar.

One of the current U.S. hurdlers wears braces and she's over 30. In fact, you can find an article about her, along with a nice picture of her holding the American flag, on the websites for many dental care offices all across the country. The article says, even though she's got an Olympic silver medal, she chooses non-metal ceramic braces. Good for her, for straightening out her teeth, I mean. Lord knows I am not implying that she's on drugs. I don't know her, and it's probably a coincidence that she's doing so well and has orthodontic issues like so many of the track stars who have come before her. Or maybe she needed another sponsor (even though she had Nike at one point) and all those dentists needed a billboard. Financially, it was probably a great deal for her. I've never seen an Olympian with braces use them like this before. I'll bet Carl Lewis and Joe Douglas wish they had thought of it.

On rare occasions, someone who runs clean takes a big chance and accuses someone else of doping. That's when the machine takes over. It destroyed Darrell Robinson. He accused Carl Lewis, Flo-Jo and others of using drugs, but he didn't have any proof other than what he says he saw. He and Carl were both members of the Santa Monica Track Club. He couldn't get any more inside access than that. When his eyewitness account wasn't enough to take down those who were deemed untouchable, Robinson suffered from the accusations. They said he was crazy. He was blacklisted and couldn't make a living because he couldn't get in a race. He was only twenty-five years old, too young to realize that no one in the big business of track and field wanted the truth to get out. The organization was the problem and he was attacking the athletes.

From what I've read, after Robinson got blacklisted from the sport, he had a troubled life and even tried committing suicide a couple of times. I don't know where he is or what he's doing because he wants it that way. He's totally off the public grid now. It's a shame. His ethics were misplaced, or rather wasted, on the wrong people and it nearly killed him.

Gwen Torrence was a star on the track at the University of Georgia and appeared in three Olympics, winning three gold medals, a silver and a bronze. She spoke out during the 1992 Games about the competitors in the women's 100 meters. Without naming names, she said only three of the eight runners in the event were clean. She didn't medal in the race and was labeled a sore loser and a crybaby for her remarks. Just like the rest of us clean runners would talk to each other, I remember she opened up to the media and said, "Everybody knows what they're doing." I could feel her frustration, from just reading the sports pages.

Because Gwen couldn't name names without offering proof, the machine attacked her. Within days the IAAF made the USOC go after Gwen to deliver a written apology to the media. She did. And the rest of us knew that was the only reason she was not suspended, blacklisted or otherwise driven off the track.

Thankfully, Gwen had other things going for her, like a real life outside of sports. I think, like me, she just endured the bedlam while she ran because she knew she would eventually move on and leave all the insanity behind. She's married, has children, and she has become a beautician and business owner in Georgia. That was her plan, even before college, and she's done it. That's success.

Harvey Glance always ran clean. He was the athlete's representative for USA Track and Field (USATF) for a while. He actually tried to do the right thing and clean it up by getting the drugs out of the sport. He got nowhere with that mission. All he got was a lot of grief from the higher-ups. Although the clean runners were ready to stand behind him, our so-called star athletes were the ones we needed. They didn't support him. A lot of us felt sorry for Harvey. In my opinion, he was the best representative we had. At least he tried. After Harvey, I don't think drugs were an issue open to discussion among the USATF big wigs.

Pauline Davis came to the University of Alabama from the Bahamas. Coach Wayne Williams says I'm the reason she chose Alabama. It was long after I left, but I guess I did help recruit her by being a good example of the kind of athlete she wanted to be. That girl worked hard and she was dedicated. She kept Alabama on the map in track and field and she competed in five Olympic Games without cheating. She's also a current member of the IAAF Council, but I can't hold that against her. She might be the one who makes a difference someday. You should see her in front of an audience of children. She's a firecracker. On the other hand, she's been with the IAAF since 2007. Knowing Pauline, this tells me that, inside the gates, cleaning up the drug problem is much more difficult than even I imagine.

Stephanie Hightower was a winner on the track as a hurdler at Ohio State in the late '70s. She suffered through the boycott of the 1980 Games and just missed making the 1984 Olympic team at the trials where so many positive tests were covered up. As one of the clean runners, she would have been on the team if those tests were revealed. She played fair and she has come up through the ranks of the organization. Stephanie has been president of the USATF since 2008 and she's also a nominee to the IAAF Council, a very powerful position in worldwide track and field. Admitting that I don't know what the world is like inside the machine, it's still hard for me to believe that I haven't seen her make a difference yet, with regards to drug use. I hope she's trying.

The IAAF, as the governing body over worldwide track and field since 1912, has had no one to answer to. They have controlled the testing, the reporting of results and the punishments for cheating. It's absolute power without any checks and balances.

Unassuming, quiet, clean-running Calvin Smith has always been outnumbered and outmatched with regards to money and power. If I spoke up about doping years ago, the International Association of Athletics Federation (IAAF), the governing body over all track and field, could have ended my career. I would have been nothing but a footnote to Ben Johnson's embarrassing Olympic moment. I was either smart enough to heed the warnings or not brave enough to try and take them on. Either way, I just kept on running, quietly. It was all I could do until now.

"The International Olympic Committee (IOC) is the supreme authority of the Olympic Movement." That's what it says on their website. And they list sixteen bullet points regarding their mission. Here's the one I find most ironic:

•   To lead the fight against doping in sport

From my point of view outside the sport now, it looks like the athletes who get into office and stay, somehow change their priorities. They get in line with what's already there. I don't see them doing anything to make the sport better. Maybe it's because in the U.S. there are so many great athletes who would like those corporate jobs in track and field. If someone makes waves, there's always another retired Olympian ready to take his place.

There were many great athletes who ran clean during my time: Mel Lattany (University of Georgia), Diane Dixson (Ohio State), Herman Frazier (Arizona State), Edwin Moses (Morehouse College), Candy Young (Farleigh-Dickinson University), Lillie Leatherwood (University of Alabama), Emmit King (University of Alabama), Willie Smith (Auburn University), Clancy Edwards (Cal Poly and USC), and Renaldo Nehemiah (University of Maryland). That's a strong crowd to run with and I'm proud to know them. And there were more. Just not many more. I hoped we would prevail someday because we were leading by example. Many years later, I take comfort in knowing we inspired some young athletes, but unfortunately not enough to turn the tide.

We weren't reaching as many people as the dopers were getting to with their performance-enhanced careers in the limelight.

You might be wondering what my friends and family were advising me to do during the years that I kept running clean, and losing to the guys who were doping. Well, except for my wife, they didn't know what was going on until they saw Daniel Gordon's documentary, 9.79 when it aired on ESPN in 2012, six years after I retired. My sister Angie has kept up with my career more than anyone in the family and she was shocked by all that she didn't know after seeing that movie.

Everybody in my world was only interested in how I did. When I lost, no one ever asked me why I got beat and I didn't made excuses. I never saw the drugs as an advantage. I saw it as cheating and I was always waiting for it to end. I'm still waiting.

During the eighties, I'd say that at least seventy percent of track and field athletes were using performance-enhancing drugs. I had the other thirty percent to talk to about it. They were already in the loop. It helped. I vented and so did they. To the outsiders, our families and fans, there was always the next race. Not knowing the situation, they didn't dwell on our losses. It wouldn't have been polite.

I complained a little to Melanie though. Well, she says it was a lot. She would tell me to keep my mouth shut and warn me I might get sued or shunned if I talked without offering up proof.

Growing up in the church, as I did, my wife has faith that those of us doing it right will eventually be rewarded and the cheaters will also get what they deserve. All final justice is in the hands of God. Melanie's mom used to say, "Whatever is done in the dark, comes to light."

My "locker" at the Mississippi Sports Hall of Fame.

The 2014 inductees to the Mississippi Sports Hall of Fame. Left to right, **Doug Cunningham** (Ole Miss, San Francisco 49ers), **me**, **Fred McNair** representing his brother Steve McNair (Alcorn State, Tennessee Titans), **Richard Williams**, Mississippi State basketball coach, **Deuce McAllister** (Ole Miss, New Orleans Saints) and **Ruthie Bolton** (Auburn University, WNBA Sacramento Monarchs).

(courtesy John Elliott *Studio*)

15

Playing Fair *IS* Winning

The public is easily swayed by winners in general. I've noticed that from being on both the inside and outside of sports.

A winning athlete who plays the God card gets a special kind love. You've seen these guys, breathless and dripping with sweat. Stick a microphone in their face and they always thank Jesus Christ himself for carrying them across the finish line. That leaves the public with the perception that this guy is a nice person who plays fair and comes out ahead by the grace of God. Those of us inside track and field know better. I'm not saying that all those who thank God for their big wins are bad people. I am saying that my God doesn't approve of winning by cheating.

The Bible says the body is the temple of the Holy Ghost. Nowhere does it say that temple can be desecrated in the pursuit of Olympic glory. These "Thank God" athletes may be nice in many areas of their lives, but if they're on the track and on steroids, they're cheating.

I remember clearly, during my running years, that people knew who the drug coaches were. And by "people," I mean all the people inside the world of track and field. If an athlete was with a coach who condoned the use of drugs, that athlete would eventually start using. Any up-and-coming athlete knew who to go to if they wanted "extra help." It was sad, very sad.

Writing this now, I realize it sounds similar to the typical story of drug addiction on the streets. It was. Only the streets I'm talking about were the best track and field facilities in the world, and the users were potentially world-class athletes who might have succeeded without the drugs. We'll never know.

What I do know is that here in the U.S., where people only notice track and field every four years, the USATF has work to do to catch up with the popularity of our sport in other parts of the world. The USOC, and every other organization that has an interest in track and field, has a responsibility to try and grow the sport in the United States. I believe that's why many athletes are allowed to do whatever it takes to become competitive as long as they win. That keeps the sponsors and fans happy and it keeps money rolling in to the sport at home.

If it weren't for my son, I wouldn't even look at track as much as I do. Because of what continues to be acceptable, it's hard to enjoy anything about it. I don't even watch the big meets on television unless Calvin II is running.

I wonder about those athletes coming back from being busted for drugs and then running faster when they return from their suspensions. It doesn't make any sense. They took drugs to run faster, got suspended for it, and now they're back with even more speed! I find it sad that most of the athletes seem to be on drugs, so I don't want to give them any more of my time.

I think a lot of the fans have caught on too. Maybe that's the reason track and field will never be one of the big sports in America. After all, we've already got millions of baseball fans who have had it with the dopers in the major leagues. They're not about to adopt another sport filled with them.

As far as I know, our country got into this doping nonsense by trying to compete with the Eastern Bloc countries. Not only were those athletes sponsored by their governments, they were clearly becoming bigger and stronger than our guys, right in front of our eyes. Heck, it looked to me like the Russian and German women were more muscular than the American men back when I was competing.

It may not have been an official declaration from the heads of state that told the coaches and doctors to experiment with drugs, but those who did were employees of the government. It seems as if their sense of nationalism and the desire to win far outweighed their sense of responsibility to the athletes.

To me, it looked as if all those Olympians were being treated like lab rats. From what I've read, the European nations were experimenting as time went on, trying this drug or that drug to make their athletes bigger, better, faster. They continued because the drugs worked, despite the side effects that might occur, and they often beat us with their new found strength and stamina. It didn't take long for the American coaches to catch on that they could shape a champion the very same way.

The Olympic Federation wants to be seen as the force that is making sports better and cleaner with the latest innovations regarding drug testing. They even started a World Anti-Doping Agency, back in 1999, which still hasn't solved the problem. I think that an entire worldwide agency dedicated to anti-doping ought to get it right. But if you scrutinize the make-up of the bureaucracy, you will see that it's funded by the IOC and participating countries. And from what I know about their rules, there are still loopholes for "cooperating athletes." The bottom line is, they created a whole new level of administration to supervise the officials who were not cleaning up sports before. Unfortunately, they're working for the same bosses who still want bigger, better and faster athletes in order to reap the financial rewards that come with winning.

As luck would have it, just before going to press with this book, the World Anti-Doping Agency (WADA) alleged that the Russian government had been complicit in sports doping. Of course, that wasn't news to me, but it did capture a few headlines. I don't think this story will go away until, well, until there is a diplomatic solution. That could take a while.

On November 10, 2015, the World Anti-Doping Agency revoked the accreditation of a Moscow anti-doping lab for allegedly covering up years of positive test results. The New York Times called it "the most extensive state-sponsored sports doping program since the 1970s." The IAAF council voted 22-1 to level tough sanctions that would keep Russia out of all international track and field events, including the 2016 Summer Olympics. It was a secret vote, and the Russian council member did not vote. I find it most interesting that someone voted not to ban them for allegedly running a doping program. According to the Associated Press, IAAF President Sebastian Coe said he is "angry" and Russia will have to fulfill a "list of criteria" to get back in the game.

Yes, I feel the Russians should be punished, but let's not stop there. They all need to hit rock bottom. Simply watching Russia go down is not going to get us there. From what I've seen and experienced throughout my career, many track and field personnel fall into the same category as the Russians. I expect the USATF (USA Track & Field) will be pointing fingers and crying outrage all the while Russia is in crisis mode. However, I think the USATF should be the last one to point a finger. We don't have any right to look down at the Russians until we're willing to look in a mirror.

The clean athletes who have represented our country in international competition, whether they have won or lost, have every right to call themselves proud Americans. But some sports organizations within this country are too proud to admit the truth; many of our top athletes and coaches, from the 1970s through the present day, are some of the worst cheaters of all time. The cover-up of the drug tests for the 1984 U.S. Olympic trials is one of the prime examples. The U.S. wasn't banned from Olympic competition after that was uncovered.

We all need to get to the truth about how doping has been accepted as the norm because everyone is doing it. But if we can eliminate doping, then — no one is doing it! Doesn't that level the playing field so that no one has an unfair advantage?

To accomplish this lofty goal of fair play, I believe we must place the responsibility for cleaning up sports into the hands of a group that has no financial ties to the outcome. The people in that group would also have to suspend their sense of nationalism. Until we find these honorable folks (extra-terrestrials?), things will probably remain tempestuous while the fox is guarding the henhouse.

Personally I think they're wasting a whole lot of time and money attacking the wrong end of the problem. Preventing the behavior might be a better place to start. You can only punish so many people without causing a collapse in the system. Look at the overcrowded prisons for an example of what doesn't work.

I don't pretend to have all the answers. But cheating to win certainly seems like a hollow victory to me. I believe most individuals understand this. It's just that when big, for-profit organizations get behind individuals, and there are high financial stakes involved, the line between right and wrong appears to get blurred.

I used to have hope that things would change. But I don't feel as positive anymore, regardless of what happens to the Russian team. I do believe there will always be clean runners who can win. I also want to believe track and field will get clean, but I doubt this will happen because the majority rules and the majority, as far as I've seen, does not really want to clean it up. They just want it to appear to be clean.

It's true these days, more athletes are being stripped of medals after the fact because of drug testing, but that does not make me happy. It would be much better if they were never awarded in the first place, because doped-up runners never should have been allowed on the track. I can only imagine how many Russian records and awards will be getting asterisks soon. As for the clean athletes, it's a disgrace that they can never get back the victories which should have been theirs. Comrades, I feel your pain.

As you have no doubt noticed, The Silent Runner I once was on the sports scene is long gone. Quiet Calvin from small-town Bolton, Mississippi is running his mouth these days. Maybe my former track mates will be surprised, but my current co-workers have only known the talkative me. (They got to this party too late.)

As I get closer to that golden age of retirement, perhaps I'll become quiet and reflective. But I wouldn't bet on it. Freedom of expression – speaking my mind – after all those years of holding back, feels great. I'm humbled by the good fortune of my life and the opportunity to tell my story. Now if I can only get that street sign they promised me....

It's been over 30 years since I was the World's Fastest Man. But I'm still the same size and weight, and for that, and much more, I'm grateful.

Track Career Highlights

Personal best   100m   9.93 (Colorado Springs 1983)
200m   19.99 (Zurich 1983)

Olympics
Gold 4 x 100m relay (Los Angeles 1984)
Bronze 100m (Seoul 1988)

World Championships
Gold 200m (Helsinki 1983)
Gold 4 x 100m relay (Helsinki 1983)
Silver 100m (Helsinki1983)
Gold 200m (Rome1987)

1992 IAAF World Cup, Havana, Cuba
Gold 4 x 100m relay
Bronze 100m

World Rankings by Track & Field News
World-ranked 10 times at 100m
World-ranked 7 times at 200m

World Records
World Record: 100 m - 9.93 (July 3, 1983)
World Record: 400 m relay - 37.86 (August 10, 1983)
World Record: 400 m relay - 37.83 (August 11, 1984)

Hall of Fame Honors
USA Track & Field Hall of Fame 2007
Mississippi Sports Hall of Fame 2014
Alabama Sports Hall of Fame 2016

Keeping Up with the Smiths

For more information on Calvin Smith and the workout regimen that made him a winner on the track, go to his Facebook page.

You can follow the next generation, Calvin Smith II at:

USA Track & Field
http://www.usatf.org

Olympics
http://www.olympic.org

International Association of Athletics Federation
http://www.iaaf.org

54551632R10101

Made in the USA
Charleston, SC
04 April 2016